An Axiological Process Ethics

An Axiological Process Ethics

Rem B. Edwards

PROCESS CENTURY PRESS
CLAREMONT, CALIFORNIA

AN AXIOLOGICAL PROCESS ETHICS
Toward Ecological Civilization Series

© 2014 Process Century Press

All rights reserved. Except for brief quotations in critical publications and reviews, no part of this book may be reproduced in any manner without prior permission from the publisher.

Process Century Press
An Imprint of the Center for Process Studies
A Program of Claremont Lincoln University &
Claremont School of Theology
1325 N. College Avenue
Claremont, CA 91711

ISBN 978-1-940447-01-8
Printed in the United States of America

Dedicated to

Charles Hartshorne, who came to Emory my senior year in college, 1955-56, and saw me through my Ph.D. degree, 1960-62.
John B. Cobb, Jr., who taught my first course in Philosophical Ethics at Emory during the winter quarter of 1956
and
My dear Mother and Grandmother
Opal Vickers Edwards
Allie Tyler Vickers

Series Preface: Toward Ecological Civilization

We live in the ending of an age. But the ending of the modern period differs from the ending of previous periods, such as the classical or the medieval. The amazing achievements of modernity make it possible, even likely, that its end will also be the end of civilization, of many species, or even of the human species. At the same time, we are living in an age of new beginnings that give promise of an ecological civilization. But its emergence is marked by a growing sense of urgency and deepening awareness that the changes must go to the roots of what has led to the current threat of catastrophe.

In June 2015, the 10th Whitehead International Conference will be held in Claremont, CA. Called "Seizing an Alternative: Toward an Ecological Civilization," it claims an organic, relational, integrated, nondual, and processive conceptuality is needed, and that Alfred North Whitehead provides this in a remarkably comprehensive and rigorous way. We propose that he can be "the philosopher of ecological civilization." With the help of those who have come to an ecological vision in other ways, the conference will explore this Whiteheadian alternative, showing how it is sufficiently advanced to provide the shared vision so urgently needed.

The judgment underlying this effort is that contemporary research and scholarship is still enthralled by the 17th-century view of nature articulated by Descartes and reinforced by Kant. Without freeing our minds of this objectifying and reductive understanding of the world, we are not likely to direct our actions wisely in response to the crisis to which this tradition has led us. Given the ambitious goal of replacing now dominant patterns of thought with one that would redirect us toward ecological civilization, clearly more is needed than a single conference. Fortunately, a larger platform is developing that inclues the conference and looks beyond it. It is named Pando Populus in honor of the world's largest and oldest organism, an aspen grove.

In preparation for the conference, and in support of the larger initiative of Pando Populus, we are publishing this series, appropriately named, "Toward Ecological Civilization."

John B. Cobb, Jr.

CONTENTS

Preface	1
1. SOULS AS FIELDS AND ACTUAL ENTITIES	11
Persons in Traditional Philosophy	12
Human and Non-human Souls	16
Bracken on Souls as Fields and Agents	20
Understanding Fields	24
Fields are Invisible, Imperceptible	24
Fields are Objectively Real	25
Fields are Physical, Spatially Extended	26
Fields Endure	28
Fields are Causes, Agents	29
An Expanded Concept of Souls as Fields	30
Souls are Invisible, Imperceptible, Self-perceptible	30
Souls are Objectively Real, Potent	31
Souls are Physical and Psychical	31
Souls are Enduring Actual Entities	32
Souls are Originative Causal Agents	34
Soul Fields, Agency, and Responsibility	35
Souls and Complete Human Beings	44
2. INTRINSIC VALUES, PERSONS, AND INDIVIDUALS	49
Intrinsically Valuable Actual Entities	49
Self-significance: Valuation of Self or by Self	49
Consciousness	54
Endurance	58
Individuality	61

Uniqueness	64
Replaceability	71
"Who or What Am I?"	74
The Value of Aggregates	84
Worldly Overvaluation of Aggregates	88
Ethical Duties to What?	91
3. THE GOOD AND THE BEAUTIFUL: ETHICS VERSUS AESTHETICS	**95**
Is Beauty Intrinsically Good?	97
Beauty Fails the Test	99
Beautiful Aggregates	102
Well-being, Good For, and Intrinsically Good	104
Pleasures and Happiness	106
Satisfactions	109
Creativity	113
Truth, Knowledge, Beliefs, Concepts	116
Self-realization	117
The Purpose of the Universe: Intensities, or Beauty	120
God's Purpose as the Intensification of Feeling	120
God's Purpose as the Creation of Beauty	124
God's Purpose as Creating Intrinsically Valuable Actual Entities	126
Is the Dispute Merely Verbal?	129
4. "GOOD," AND WHAT AND HOW WE VALUE	**133**
Defining "Good"	133
The Form of the Good	136
Defining "Better," "Best," and "Ought"	143
Three Dimensions of Goodness: Systemic, Extrinsic, and Intrinsic	145
Moore's Principle of Isolation	148

The Hierarchy of Value	151
Value Combinations and Confusions	154
Valuations, Or How We value	156
Valuing Good Things in Different Dimensions	163
5. DEGREES, ETHICS, AND VIRTUE	169
Degrees of Intrinsic Worth, Marginal Cases, and Animals	169
Abortion	173
Terminal Cases	176
Unrelievable Suffering	177
Animals	179
Intrinsic, Moral, and Spiritual Goodnes	181
Three Dimensions of Ethics and Virtue	182
Systemic Ethics and Systemic Virtues	184
Extrinsic Ethics and Extrinsic Virtues	191
Intrinsic Ethics and Intrinsic Virtues	197
Major Obstacles to Virtuous Living	205
Ethical and Spiritual Values and Evaluations	209
Works Cited	219
About the Author	225

PREFACE

For many years I have been thinking off and on about how to combine and harmonize two philosophical perspectives that have greatly influenced me—process philosophy and Hartmanian formal axiology. Chronologically, process philosophy came first. In the 1950s and early 1960s, I was a student of Charles Hartshorne and John B. Cobb, Jr. at Emory University, and of Robert L. Calhoun and many other theological luminaries at Yale University Divinity School. After receiving my Ph.D. in philosophy from Emory in 1962, I taught for four years at Jacksonville University in Florida. I then joined the University of Tennessee philosophy faculty in 1966. The following year, Robert S. Hartman came to teach in our department for a half-year at a time, the other half being spent at the National University of Mexico in Mexico City.

While he was with us, and for many years thereafter, I was probably Hartman's most severe critic. Yet I was greatly intrigued by his teachings and sat in as a junior colleague on almost all of his graduate courses. Fifteen years or so after his death, I finally figured out that his most powerful insights into what and how we value could be cleanly separated from other parts with which I strongly disagree to this day (Edwards 2010, 67-81). His formal axiology is the best thing I have ever found for making sense of what and how we should value. Over the years, his ways of thinking about human values and valuations have slowly transformed my own thinking, acting, feeling, and total personal outlook—though I still have a long way to go in moral and spiritual self-development. In very recent years, I have published two books applying this axiology to what I call "identification spirituality" (Edwards 2012, a and b). This book concentrates on ethics but returns to spirituality toward the end.

In this book I propose to show that process philosophy and Hartmanian formal axiology are natural partners, that they should be united, and that both would be greatly strengthened by such a union. Process ethics may have the most to gain. I hope to make a plausible case for this, but first another historical note. This is not the first encounter of the two. In the 1960s, Charles Hartshorne and Robert S. Hartman were very much in contact with each other. In his *Anselm's Discovery* (261-65), Hartshorne replied to Hartman's article on the ontological argument. Very soon after Hartman published *The Structure of Value* in 1967, Hartshorne sent to John W. Davis, then our philosophy department head at the University of Tennessee, a brochure about the graduate program in philosophy at the University of Texas. Handwritten by Hartshorne at the bottom of the page were these words: "I've been reading R.S.H. Fantastically ingenious and challenging" (Hartman 1995, 54, 125). In 1965 and 1967, Hartshorne wrote two letters to Hartman asking him to clarify his position on certain issues like God's necessary existence and the temporality of the human self, and Hartman wrote a response to him that I published in *Formal Axiology and Its Critics* (Edwards 1995, 56-61).

When John Cobb set out to explain process ethics in 1965, he recognized, "There is a range of ethical questions on which he [Whitehead] throws only indirect light," and he acknowledged the necessity of "supplementing his work by treating questions neglected by him" (1965, 113). Now, in 2013, the same insights apply to the current state of process ethics. By adding motifs developed in this book to process ethics as it now stands, a new and much stronger axiological process ethics results. The first three chapters of this book identify what I believe to be weaknesses in the current state of process ethics and develop ways of compensating for them.

The fourth and fifth chapters explain that and how formal axiology can add depth to process ethics, given its neglected themes.

Chapter One develops a process/axiological analysis of "soul" or "self." Process thinkers heavily emphasize the *temporal and relational* aspects of human selfhood, and Robert S. Hartman heavily emphasized the intrinsic worth of unique, *enduring,* embodied human selves. Human endurance should be united more forcefully and convincingly with the transience of human experience. Change of soul is important, but so is some degree of constancy. Chapter One argues that these two emphases belong harmoniously together and complete one another's inadequacies. In real people, endurance is united with transience.

This chapter further develops and builds upon Joseph A. Bracken's profound insight that the metaphysics of unique, conscious, enduring, active, and responsible souls is best understood by analogy with the physical or psycho/physical concept of a "field." Going beyond Bracken, fields are imperceptible to our ordinary senses, or in the mode of presentational immediacy. Fields are nevertheless very real and are not just conceptual constructs having no reference to reality. They are physical in the sense of being spatially extended. They endure, unlike actual occasions, and they are efficient causes or agents. Whitehead's concept of "souls" as the enduring actualities in our bodies is then re-analyzed in light of these properties of fields. The result is that enduring souls, not just fleeting actual occasions, are fundamental enduring actual entities and agents. Contrary to Whitehead and most process thinkers, actual occasions are not the only fundamental actual entities and agents within our universe. The embodiment and psycho/physicality of all souls, human, animal, and Divine, are heavily emphasized and pushed as far as possible into the depths of nature, the great chain of becoming—to plants, cells, atoms, waves, sub-atomic particles, and beyond. A more careful panexperientialist account is given of the physicality of souls, which is what enables them to interact with their own brains and bodies.

Chapter Two begins with an analysis of Whitehead's own understanding of "intrinsic importance" as "self-significance." As the central defining property of "intrinsic goodness," "self-significance" is interpreted to mean "valuing self or others." Self-significance presupposes other properties that are also essential for defining "intrinsically good." This chapter makes them explicit—consciousness or awareness, endurance, individuality, and uniqueness. The outcome is that all and only unique enduring individuals that are self- or other-valuing and conscious or experiencing are intrinsically valuable.

A serious ambiguity in Whitehead's understanding of what counts as an "individual" is exposed. He called both fleeting actual occasions and enduring souls "individuals," but he regarded only actual occasions as metaphysically and axiologically basic. He wrote of "the importance of the individual" (*AI* 292), but which kind of "individual" did he have in mind? Probably only the former—actual occasions. This chapter argues that it should have been the latter—unique, individual, enduring, valuing agents or subjects.

The replaceability of all non-intrinsic values without loss of worth, and the non-replaceability of all intrinsic values, are explained. Uniqueness makes the difference. A process/axiological answer to "Who am I?" is developed. We are both enduring soul-fields and our ever-expanding "total property inventory." Time is perpetual creation as well as perpetual perishing. The proper instrumental value of "material goods," or "aggregates," that is, of mindless or internally vacuous macroscopic physical sensory objects like cars, buildings, land, etc., is discussed. Why so many "worldly" people overvalue such things is also explained, along with our proper indirect ethical duties toward and with them.

Chapter Three examines what should be several lively and unresolved controversies in process ethics. Which is axiologically the most fundamental, ethics or aesthetics? Do beauty and other aesthetic values have intrinsic worth? Do only aesthetic values, but not unique valuing subjects, have intrinsic worth? Hedonists claim that only pleasure is intrinsically good, and Kant claimed that respecting persons as ends means only respecting the moral law within them, so both valued unique human beings only extrinsically, that is, as useful containers for holding pleasure or the moral law. With its emphasis on the intrinsic goodness of beauty, is process ethics in the same boat? Are unique conscious subjects valuable only as useful receptacles for containing beauty or other aesthetic values? Does beauty really fulfill the defining properties of "intrinsically good"? This chapter distinguishes between being "intrinsically good" and being "good for" intrinsically valuable actual entities. It argues that most values heavily emphasized by Whitehead and other process ethicists are only "good for" us, even when they exist only within us.

This chapter contends that beauty, pleasure, happiness, satisfaction, creativity, truth, knowledge, beliefs, concepts, and self-realization are universals, eternal objects, that could not be ends to, for, or by themselves. They do not exemplify the defining properties of "intrinsically good." They could not be valuable "for their own sakes" because they have no "sakes," no self-significance. They are not unique, experiencing, conscious, enduring selves or other valuing actual entities. They are immensely good for us, but not in, to, or for themselves. They know nothing, are conscious of nothing, feel nothing, value nothing, and nothing is meaningful to them. They are meaningful and valuable only to and for us and other unique non-human valuing subjects like the animals.

The chapter also critically examines the widely held process views that either the intensification of feeling or the creation of beauty is the purpose of the universe, God's own purpose for the universe. Serious weaknesses of these claims are exposed, and a different understanding of God's aim for the universe is proposed. God's purpose should be reconceived as: Creating an endless array of unique valuing subjects whose lives are constantly being enriched by innumerable "good for" properties. These are beneficial eternal objects like beauty, creativity, enjoyment, love, compassion, self-realization, etc. Logically, this could take place either in superspace or supertime, perhaps both. Serious difficulties with assuming an infinite number of antecedent universes, each created out of the chaos of its predecessor, are briefly explained. The outcome is that both process ethics and process theology should make ethics rather than aesthetics axiologically fundamental.

Chapter Four explains Hartmanian axiology's potential contributions to the currently incomplete state of process ethics. Throughout this chapter and the next, undeveloped or underdeveloped themes in current process ethics are identified and related to better developed motifs in formal axiology. What are some of these?

First, Hartmanian axiology can bring much needed order and clarity to process thought about how to define "good," "better," and "best" in a formal way that avoids G.E. Moore's "naturalistic fallacy." This really is a fallacy, despite some current doubts about it. Process ethicists use these axiological concepts profusely, but they never define them or analyze their meaning and uses. Hartman's "Good is concept fulfillment" means that value objects are good if they exemplify the descriptive "good making properties" contained within the conceptual standards or ideal concepts (norms) being applied to them. They are good if they actually have *all* the properties they are supposed to have, if they actually fulfill or measure up to all the ideal predicates contained within their relevant norms. Such norms or standards may contain an indefinite number of ideal good-making predicates. If entities being evaluated exemplify these ideal properties to some *lesser degree,* they are only fair, average, poor, or no good. The goodness of *anything* can be measured by comparing its actual properties with its ideal predicates. This works for a good God, a good religion, a morally good person, a good car, a good business, a good bargain, a good theory or belief, or a good anything. Clarity about this "Form of the Good" can help resolve many axiological disagreements, but not all. This formal definition of "good" is objective in theory yet subjective in application. We may disagree about or misunderstand relevant good-making properties, or we may make mistakes in correlating facts with ideals. "Subjective aims" can be formulated and assessed rationally. Affections or feelings are involved in selecting good-making properties.

Second, Hartmanian axiology pays more careful attention to *what* we value. It recognizes three basic kinds or dimensions of goodness, intrinsic (e.g., people and animals), extrinsic (e.g., useful material things or aggregates), and systemic (e.g., systems, beliefs, doctrines, rules, etc.). Because some of these axiological dimensions have a greater quantity or quality of good-making properties than others, they fall into a logical hierarchy of degrees of value. Qualities may be more important than sheer quantities. Thus, intrinsic goods are richer in good-making properties than, thus better than, extrinsic goods, and for the same reason extrinsic goods have more worth than mere thoughts or beliefs about extrinsic and intrinsic goods. In application, people (or animals, etc.) are more valuable than good things or aggregates, and good things are more valuable than our conceptual symbols for them and for people or animals. Value combinations, and complications with respect to these themes, are explored.

Third, formal axiology attends more carefully to how we value (valuation) than standard process ethics. We can value anything in any dimension of value in three different ways, that is, systemically or disinterestedly, extrinsically or with ordinary everyday desires and interests, and intrinsically with great passion and intensity. In all such instances, we can be guided rationally or conceptually by the Form of the Good. The contents of that form become richer in good-making properties as we progress from the systemic to the extrinsic to the intrinsic.

Chapter Five first explores vexing issues raised by degrees of intrinsic worth in "marginal cases," in our ethical relations with animals, and in killing, death, and dying. Then, three axiological approaches to ethics itself and ethical virtues are explained.

Systemic ethics emphasizes conceptual ideals and formal principles, rules, and regulations. Some ethical theories (e.g., Kant's) have been primarily if not exclusively systemic. Problems here include how to word ethical ideals and maxims properly, how to make exceptions to moral rules, and how to correct inadequacies in what Whitehead regarded as outmoded but widely accepted moral codes. *Systemic virtues* or dispositions include love of truth and knowledge, impartially or disinterestedness, curiosity or wonder, and intellectual honesty, modesty, and humility. Such intellectual virtues may spill over into and be applied to morality itself. Both Whitehead and Hartman exhibited these virtues.

Extrinsic ethics includes systemic considerations, moral beliefs, but it emphasizes mainly actions and consequences rather moral rules. It is a minimalistic practical ethics for ordinary people, not the maximizing intrinsic ethics of saints and heroes. It is adopted for its usefulness with respect to personal good or the common good. The two are conflated in long range egoism, reciprocal altruism, and social contract ethics. Its ethical requirements are the socially enforceable minimal civilities, decencies, practices, and duties that are normally required for worthwhile personal and social living. Extrinsic duties include respect for and observance of the most basic human laws and rights, but extrinsic ethics does not require maximally oriented moral actions and affections or the extraordinary virtues of saints and heroes. It does not moralize the whole of life. Its moral virtues are very commonplace pro-social temperaments essential for just getting along, the ones that can be expected to pay off to oneself in the long run. "Honesty pays," and "Every good deed will be rewarded." *Extrinsic virtues* are grounded in reciprocal altruism and the lowly self-interested social contract: "I won't hurt you if you won't hurt me; I will help you if you will help me." Extrinsic ethics and its virtues are applied mainly to local "in groups," for they are ones most likely to provide help to oneself when needed. Outsiders and inferiors are beyond the pale of moral concern and obligation.

Intrinsic ethics, by contrast, is a maximizing ethics that aims for optimum good for everyone. It is more intense, unselfish, and universalistic than extrinsic ethics. It goes "beyond the call of duty" when this is called for by *intrinsic virtues* like genuinely altruistic love, empathy, and compassion. It is the passionate and intense morality of saints and heroes. It takes very seriously the intrinsic worth not only of every unique human being but also every unique animal and every living thing affected by what we do. It also rejoices in the existence and inherent goodness of those we cannot directly influence, whether in the past, on the other side of the world, or in galaxies far far away. Its scope is universal; it is not limited to insiders or by any form of parochialism or snobbery. This virtuous way of life aims at maximum goodness for and minimum harm to everyone and everything. Its moral community is global, and beyond. Whitehead's was a maximizing ethics, and so was Hartman's. Several major obstacles to virtuous living are identified and discussed, for example, undervaluing or disvaluing people and animals, and the "insider/outsider" distinction. The chapter concludes by exploring how ethical and spiritual values and virtues tend to merge at the apex of moral and spiritual development.

Many themes in the last two chapters of this book have been much neglected, but not completely so, by previous process ethicists. Process ethics can and will become much more appealing and persuasive if these neglected themes from Hartmanian formal axiology are added to it, yielding an axiological process ethics. Much more relevant information about Robert S. Hartman and formal axiology is made available by the Robert S. Hartman Institute on line at: <www.hartmaninstitute.org>.

Modified sections of previously published articles have been integrated into this book here and there. The first two paragraphs of this preface illustrate this. They come from my "People and Their Worth: Uniting Process and Axiology," *Process Studies* 38:1 (2009): 43-68. Other modified sections were taken from my "Toward an Axiological Virtue Ethics," in the *Quarterly of Ethical Research*, 2013: 25-60, an Islamic philosophy journal sponsored by the departments of theology and philosophy at the University of Qom, Iran.

The abbreviations for Whitehead's books used in the references are given in the "Works Cited" near the end of the book.

Short quotes in this book from several sources fall within the realm of "fair use," but I would like to thank the following publishers for their explicit permission to use more extensive previously published material:

University Press of America for quotes from Rem B. Edwards, *The Essentials of Formal Axiology*.

Simon & Schuster for quotes from these books by Alfred North Whitehead: *Science and the Modern World, Process and Reality, Adventures of Ideas,* and *Modes of Thought*.

Daniel A. Dombrowski, Editor, for rewritten passages from Rem B. Edwards, "People and Their Worth: Uniting Process and Axiology." *Process Studies* 38.1 (2009): 43-68.

Alireza Sayadmansour, Editor, for rewritten passages from Rem B. Edwards, "Toward an Axiological Virtue Ethics," *Quarterly of Ethical Research* (2013): 25-60.

1.

SOULS AS FIELDS AND ACTUAL ENTITIES

Immanuel Kant had the right words for it: Our ethical duty is to treat persons always as ends in themselves and never merely as means (52-53). Just what Kant meant by this, however, is highly suspect. Without being inconsistent with his own metaphysics, he was not talking about real people who we *experience* in space and time, for we are mere appearances, he thought. He must have been talking about noumenal egos that have no spatial or temporal properties whatsoever, and to which the categories of cause and effect do not apply. People that we encounter in space and time, either through sensory perception or through the self-consciousness that Alfred North Whitehead called "direct awareness of ourselves" (*PR* 107), are mere illusions, not realities, according to Kant's purportedly non-metaphysical metaphysics. As Whitehead observed, for Kant, "No element in the temporal world could itself be an experient. His temporal world . . . was in its essence dead, phantasmal, phenomenal" (*PR* 190).

One of the many reasons why I am a Whiteheadian (slightly heretical) and not a Kantian is that we think, or should think, that all unique and unified individual subjects or enduring souls—people, animals, and beyond—have intrinsic worth and ought to be treated as ends and not merely as means to our own private, personal, or human objectives. Another reason is that we believe that people, animals, and living things in space and time are real, not merely phenomenal appearances, and we also know how to apply notions of cause and effect to ourselves and others without lapsing into rigid determinism. We can conceive of the very real decisions that we *experience* ourselves as making in time as having necessary but not sufficient antecedent causal conditions that leave room for creativity and freedom, and as having real effects upon our future selves and other spatiotemporally real selves, whether human, sub-human, or Divine. That has great significance for ethics as well as for theology.

All of this raises some important questions. What resources are available to us in process thought for conceiving of individual enduring persons as responsible agents, and for regarding and treating persons and other enduring souls as intrinsically valuable, as ends in themselves? What exactly is a "person" or an "individual" having moral standing on Whiteheadian grounds? For simplicity we will deal mainly with human beings at first, but keep in mind that what we discover will also apply by degrees to all non-human individuals in *the great chain of becoming*. We will later return to animals and other individual subjects of experience.

PERSONS IN TRADITIONAL PHILOSOPHY

We learn to distinguish between "people" or "persons," "cats," "rocks," and "words" as we grow up. All of these are value-laden ordinary language concepts. All human concepts are value-laden teleological instruments. Philosophers and theologians attempt to refine ordinary understanding using special philosophical or theological jargon. As Whitehead said, "Thus the very purpose of philosophy is to delve below the apparent clarity of common speech" (*AI* 222).

In traditional non-process philosophy, individual persons are technically defined in terms of "substances" and "attributes," following Aristotle and Boethius, who defined a "person" as an "individual substance of a rational nature" (84-85). Traditionally, rationality, as Aristotle said, was the essential defining attribute of human substances: "Man is a rational animal." Substances as such cannot be experienced. They are the enduring, self-sufficient, unchanging, individual realities to which all predicates/properties/qualities/relations (like rationality) belong. Substances as such have only a few skimpy properties of their own: self-sufficiency (despite our obvious contingency), endurance, changelessness, and foundational support for and ownership of changing qualities and relations. For the most part, they are just "supposed somethings we know not what," as John Locke put it. Substances and their skimpy properties are never given to us in experience, as David Hume correctly indicated. "Substance," like "unicorn" is an intension without a corresponding extension. It is a vacuous conceptual construct, an instance of Whitehead's "misplaced concreteness," which consists of "mistaking the abstract for the concrete" (*SMW* 51).

The traditional substance/attribute perspective affirms that all of us are the same changeless individual substances from birth to death, though many of our attributes (except for our "essences," e.g., "rationality," or "character") are in a state of flux throughout our lives, some more so than others. Even rationality and character are not really as constant as they were once cracked up to be. We are only intermittently conscious and rational, and we are often out of character, as Whitehead well understood. Self-identical individuality through time is absolute in substance and essence, according to traditional non-process philosophy. Dualistic Platonic/Cartesian philosophies further distinguish between mental and material substances, identifying "self" only with non-spatial mental or conscious thinking substances that are imprisoned in alien material or spatially extended bodies.

Process thought challenges traditional substance/attribute, mind/body dualisms. No absolutely enduring substances or essences exist; people are incredibly complex embodied causally linked and temporally sequenced sets of concretizing happenings in time (events, actual occasions) in which eternal objects or properties/predicates inhere momentarily, perish, and transmit what they can of themselves into their immediate temporal successors.

This chapter challenges Whitehead's reduction of "soul" or "self" to the mere sum of the actual occasions in our stream of consciousness from birth to death. It argues that individual souls are more than this. We are embodied enduring relational and contingent soul-fields. We are more than the mere sum of the actual occasions in our stream of consciousness, though these are also included in our total reality. There are no enduring, changeless, and self-sufficient substances, but we are embodied, changing, contingent, relational, but relatively enduring and active soul-fields.

Considering nothing more than the properties of our present personalities, we are only relatively the same persons today that we were ten years ago, for many of our character traits (concretized universals or eternal objects) have changed, while others persist. "Substance" (with its skimpy properties) is not one of *our* properties at any stage along life's way. Repudiating substances in general involves rejecting both the distinction between mental and material substances, and the depreciation or devaluation of embodiment that typically accompanies it. In process thought, consciousness or mentality (broadly understood) in human beings is inherently embodied, and that is not a bad thing. Bodies are not bad. Bodies are good. At fundamental levels, all spatially extended entities have psychological properties, and all psychological entities have spatial properties. Because the primary emphasis of process thought is on time rather than space, mind/body dualism can be avoided without getting rid of either minds or bodies. All temporal actualities are both spatially extended and psychologically structured or endowed.

Traditional philosophical empiricists were psychologically hung up on space. This is why they recognized the reality and validity only of external sense experiences and the material world. People, they say, are only material beings having merely those sets of extrinsic properties that are given to us through our ordinary external senses of touch, sight, hearing, taste, and smell. By contrast, in process thought experience is primarily temporal. Our most basic or primitive experiences are temporal, subjective, psychological, and internal, not external, spatial, and sensory. Whitehead held that receiving data and subjective forms (e.g., consciousness, memories, purposes, feelings, thoughts, etc.) from the immediate temporal predecessors of our momentarily existing selves is the most basic form of human experience (*AI* 180-84). He called this "perception in the mode of causal efficacy." Time, no matter how it is analyzed, is metaphysically and experientially fundamental. However, becoming consciously aware of this seems to require some special philosophical or spiritual talent and personal self-development. Most people do not focus on perception in the mode of causal efficacy. Most dwell on external sensory spatial perception "in the mode of presentational immediacy," as Whitehead termed it. Space is integral to time, and time to space, hence "spacetime" rather than "space" versus "time."

Persons, as next explained, are relatively enduring embodied soul-fields that include within themselves temporally ordered societies of successive and causally connected spacetime occurrences or occasions of self-experience, self-valuation, creativity, and freedom. A single person's soul consists largely of a vast connected chain or stream of causally and creatively ordered successive occasions, but more than that, it endures, so this chapter argues. Included are consciousness, bodily awareness, sensations, free choices, thoughts, feelings, creative syntheses, and the determinate universals or eternal objects that belong to that stream. The stream of consciousness, the dominant temporally ordered society or actual entity within the human body, is only the tip of the iceberg, though no less valuable for being so, and *the rest of the iceberg is made out of the same stuff,* as are all icebergs. All bodily cells are also actively experiencing and processing actualities.

A complete person consists of all of her or his properties from birth to death, whether they be fields, occasions, qualities, relations, experiences, psychological, physical, conscious, unconscious, thinking, feeling, creative, or whatever. Our human properties are not exclusively spatial, sensory, and internally vacuous. About this, Hartmanian axiologists and process thinkers agree. This enables both to make a legitimate place for what Hartman would call systemic and intrinsic, in addition to extrinsic, personal properties and values. We must begin with Whitehead's understanding of souls.

HUMAN AND NON-HUMAN SOULS

To understand Whitehead's view of persons, the most obvious place to start, and it is only a start, is with his view that the "soul of man" is the "dominant 'personal' society of occasions" within the human body (*AI* 211, 290; *PR* 109, 119). The human soul is more than a random "society of occasions." It is personally ordered, which means that its members succeed one another in time in "a single line of inheritance." It is also an "enduring object," which means that its members inherit from their predecessors "a common element of form," or "a defining characteristic" (*PR* 34)—for example, "emotional forms" (114), "subjective forms" (233-35), "subjective aims" (85), "consciousness" (*AI* 231), etc. "We," said Whitehead, are "enduring objects with personal order" (*PR* 161). Expressed more simply and clearly, our self-identity through time consists in the persistence of our character or personality traits. We are the same person that we were last year to the extent that we have the same feelings, interests, desires, emotions, beliefs, dispositions, habits, behaviors, etc.

So, a human soul or person is an enduring object, a society of actual occasions, with sustained subjective psychological properties or subjective forms, including intermittent consciousness and rationality (*PR* 79, 108, 161-62, 177; *AI* 269-70, 183-84, 186-88, 291; *MT* 162-63). According to Whitehead, "There are many species of subjective forms, such as emotions, valuations, purposes, adversions, aversions, consciousness, etc." (*PR* 24). Whitehead's concept of an *"enduring object" as a society* must be explored more thoroughly and perhaps modified if we are to make a place in process thought for persons and other enduring individuals as agents and ends in themselves. We must ask, first, what kind of *reality* do persons as enduring societies have, and, second, what kind of *value* do persons as enduring societies have? This chapter deals with the first question. The next chapter covers the second.

What kind of reality does a human soul have? Whitehead understood the soul to be an *enduring object* composed entirely of a society of successive actual occasions. About this, some questions must be raised. Is this society *merely the sum total* of the successive evanescent occasions that compose it? Or does the soul have some kind of *reality and power* that its transient temporal constituents do not have? Is the soul an organic whole which is more than the sum of its parts? Do soul-societies of actual occasions have emergent properties and powers of their own? Can souls *do* anything that their individual occasions cannot do? Do actual occasions in our streams of consciousness do things that our souls do not do? Do souls have any kind of *value* that their individual occasions do not have? Do we have moral obligations to souls that we do not have to actual occasions?

Whitehead said many things indicating that enduring objects, including human souls, are nothing more than the additive totality of their constituent occasions, and that they do not have any distinctive reality, power, properties, or worth of their own. Do enduring unique human individuals, as we ordinarily conceive of them, have intrinsic worth in Whiteheadian ethics and metaphysics? Neither Whitehead nor Kant may have meant by "individual" what we ordinarily mean for ethical purposes. For Kant, individual persons in time and space are mere appearances or phenomena, not realities. For Whitehead, enduring people seem to be only relatively lasting societies, not real individuals or agents at all, especially so if reality and agency belong *only* to their constituent temporal occasions. Many Whiteheadian texts, given next, suggest that only actual occasions are real individuals with power and worth.

First, some Whiteheadian texts clearly identify enduring human souls or personalities with their component occasions, or with nothing more than certain formal properties common to them:

> The enduring personality is the historic route of living occasions which are severally dominant in the body at successive instants. (*PR* 119)

> An enduring personality in the temporal world is a route of occasions in which the successors with some peculiar completeness sum up their predecessors. (350)

> What endures is identity of pattern, self-inherited. (*SMW* 194)

> Endurance is the property of finding its pattern reproduced. (152)

Second, actual occasions are the only truly real things in the universe:

> 'Actual entities'—also termed 'actual occasions'—are the final real things of which the world is made up. There is no going behind actual entities to find anything more real. (*PR* 18)

> This interplay [of subject with object] is the stuff constituting those individual things which make up the sole reality of the

Universe. These individual things are the individual occasions of experience, the actual entities. (*AI* 177, 294)

I have termed each individual act of immediate self-enjoyment an *occasion of experience*. I hold that these unities of existence, these occasions of experience, are the really real things. (*MT* 151)

Third, since being is power, as Plato said (*AI* 120), and enduring souls have no fundamental being of their own, it follows that they have no power of their own.

[A] society is only efficient through its individual members. (*PR* 91)

Agency belongs exclusively to actual occasions. (31)

The "Editors' Notes" to *Process and Reality* suggest that Whitehead would ascribe agency to God as a single everlasting and continuously concresceing actual entity (395), but Whitehead never indicated that enduring human souls are agents. More about God and our souls' resemblance to God will come later.

Such pronouncements invite an important question. If only individuals have agency and intrinsic worth, and if only actual occasions count as individuals, do only occasions, but not enduring souls, have moral responsibilities and intrinsic worth? All of the preceding pronouncements clearly weigh heavily against the reality, agency, ontological continuity through time, and intrinsic worth of enduring souls or persons. More documentation on the intrinsic worth part will be given in the next chapter. As explained later, the issue of the value of individuals is complicated by the fact that Whiteheadians often treat soul-societies, and not just actual occasions, as individuals, but only in a secondary sense, and perhaps only as a concession to ordinary language. The fact remains that for Whitehead only actual occasions are primary individuals. Process thinkers may need to develop concepts of "soul" and "person" that go beyond Whitehead if they are to make a place for recognizing and treating enduring persons and other enduring individuals as agents and as ends in themselves.

BRACKEN ON SOULS AS FIELDS AND AGENTS

Joseph A. Bracken, a very innovative process thinker, moved significantly beyond Whitehead's interpretation of the metaphysical status of enduring soul-objects by allowing them some small degree of agency, as in his 1989 article, "Energy-Events and Fields" (153-65). This theme was carried forward in many of his subsequent articles and books. Bracken agreed that on the basis of Whitehead's own words every society "appears to be nothing more than the sum of its parts," and that each soul is only "an aggregate of actual occasions possessing a 'common element of form'" (153).

In his 2002 article, "Continuity Amid Discontinuity: A Neo-Whiteheadian Understanding of Self," Bracken asked, "What is the nature or deeper reality of a Whiteheadian society? If it is not an aggregate of actual occasions, what is it?" (119) In answering, here and in several other publications, Bracken moved beyond Whitehead in two important ways. First he applied the concept of "field" to enduring objects like human souls. Second, he assigned a small degree of independent and non-reductive reality and originative causality to enduring souls as such. If, as Bracken proposed, human souls are fields that are more than the mere sum of their parts, what more, and what does that mean? Organic wholes and organisms are more than the sum of their parts. This means that the whole either has shared properties *larger* than the sum of those of its members, or else that it has *additional* properties not possessed by its members. How does this apply to fields, and to Whitehead's souls?

As for *fields,* Whitehead was definitely familiar with the concept. He mentioned fields with some frequency in his writings, (*CN* 78, 170,181, 190; *SMW* 102, 129, 132, 132-36, *IS* 17, 67, 133, 135; *AE* 151-53; *PR* 80, 92, 98, 333; *AI* 156, 157). He said, "The whole spatial universe is a field of force, or in other words, a field of incessant activity" (*MT* 136). He wrote of "a field of physical activity pervading all space" (*SMW* 98) and of "an electromagnetic field of activity pervading space and time" (152). He recognized that "electromagnetic effects were conceived as arising from a continuous field" (99) and that "happenings in that field . . . are divorced from immediate dependence upon matter" (102). He even spoke of "the perceptual field" (91) and "the psychological field" (194), but he never made much of fields metaphysically. Most importantly, he did not take Bracken's step of treating enduring objects like human souls as fields.

Bracken hesitantly assigned a derivative but more-than-additive reality and causality to enduring souls as fields, but he seems both to deny and affirm this. "My own position," he wrote, "is to affirm with Whitehead that agency in the strict sense belongs exclusively to actual occasions, but also to claim that the effect of the interrelated agencies of the occasions within a society is to produce a collective agency necessary for the society to preserve its pattern of order or ongoing self-identity from moment to moment" (1989, 156). Thereafter "collective agency" appears several times (157), but this sounds almost like an oxymoron, given Whitehead's insistence that only actual occasions are agents and are finally real, and Bracken's own "agency in the strict sense belongs exclusively to actual occasions."

Just what kind of reality and "collective agency" do societies as enduring objects have? This issue is especially acute when considering human and animal souls, their value, and their agency. Whiteheadian souls are collections of actual occasions that share inherited subjective forms, but are they merely that? Are they also organic wholes or subjects having powers and an ongoing self-identity that actual occasions do not have either individually or collectively? Are they subjects and agents in themselves or as such? Are the choices they make identical with and reducible to the choices of their ingredient actual occasions? Or not so?

Deliberately moving beyond Whitehead, Bracken hesitantly identified enduring societal soul-fields as unified subjects and agents having causal effectiveness, specifically, the power to preserve their own identity through time. In his 2002 article, Bracken said, "All these interrelated agencies of actual occasions fuse into a collective agency operative at the level of the society as a whole," and a collective society "is a higher level ontological totality with a collective agency proper to itself which, at the same time, is derivative from the interrelated agencies of its constituent actual occasions" (120). But what exactly are the powers of this collective agency, and does it have any powers of its own that are not "derivative" from its constituent occasions?

In a 2004 essay, Bracken defined "society" as "a structured field of activity for its constituent 'actual occasions' or momentary subjects" (212). He identified his "own contribution to Whiteheadian scholarship" as the idea that "a field could well serve as the process-relational equivalent of substance in classical metaphysics, that which endures over time and undergoes accidental modifications" (214). Yet, he also denies the distinctive agency of collective societies as fields, claiming that they are "passive rather than active," and that the agency of a field is "the collective agency of all the constituent actual occasions working in unison rather than the agency of a single organizing principle" (214). This sure sounds like "mere addition" to me!

In a later book, Bracken affirmed that collective societies are "structured fields of activity" (2006, 9), and that although a field is "semipermanent," it has "some reality proper to itself" and "can give order and coherence" to its occasions. Yet, it is not "a still higher subject of experience" (106). This still leaves us wondering just what his collective-agency soul-fields are, what they can actually do that their ingredient occasions do not do, and why they are anything more than the mere sum of their parts.

I want to go beyond Bracken and affirm unequivocally that *enduring soul-fields as such have a fundamental reality, agency, and value of their own.* Whitehead regarded only two things, actual occasions and God, as fundamentally real actual entities. I propose a third: *Enduring human and animal souls are also fundamentally real actual entities.* Whitehead may never have called them "individuals," but let's make them real *primary* individuals. Perhaps there are more finally real things in the universe than were dreamed of in Whitehead's philosophy, and this has great significance for process ethics.

I will next try to explain that and how human and animal souls are indeed "still higher subjects of experience," contrary to Bracken. Then I will identify some of the real powers of, and establish the intrinsic goodness of, enduring souls. Why stop where Bracken does? Why so limit or be so unclear and hesitant about the full actuality and powers of ourselves as enduring souls as fields? If self-experience shows that we as human souls can do nothing more than merely preserve our own self-identity, then we should accept Bracken's limitations to "preserving its own identity" and being "an organizing field." What if experiential knowledge of both self and fields discloses much more about what we are and can do? What if immediate self-experience discloses that we can also directly and deliberately influence and to some degree control what transpires within our soul fields, and beyond? What if it shows that the occasions within our stream of consciousness are not the only agents, but we as enduring souls are also creative and responsible agents? What if it shows not only that our occasions have transient self valuation but that *in addition* we as enduring souls have much more permanent self-valuation?

UNDERSTANDING FIELDS

As a way of getting to the "more" of enduring selves, the general concept of a "physical field" must be examined in greater depth. Bracken was on the right track, but he did not go quite far enough. In introducing fields as distinctive realities into Whiteheadian metaphysics, perhaps Bracken gave us much more than he realized. But what? He took the first steps in giving to all of philosophy a new way to solve the mind-body problem and the personal identity problem. Here are a few relevant things that we need to understand about physical fields if we are to go beyond Bracken.

FIELDS ARE INVISIBLE, IMPERCEPTIBLE

Physical fields as such are "invisible," indeed *imperceptible* to *any* of our "external senses." Only their effects are perceptible. In this respect, physical fields are like the theologians' "spirits" and their invisible God, "the soul of the universe" (John Wesley). They are also like the invisible minds or "mental substances" of Platonism and Descartes. Before the Logical Positivists' "Principle of Verification" (statements are meaningful only if they have direct sensory import) was ever formulated, natural science had already moved far beyond recognizing only sensory concepts and propositions as meaningful. Scientists like Einstein were employing concepts of physical but non-sensory realities and making statements about imperceptible physical forces and processes that were properly scientific, meaningful, and true or false. Both scientists and theologians regularly appeal to things unseen to explain things that are seen.

Natural science is often defined as appealing only to sensory experiences for its affirmations, but that is not what practicing scientists actually do, even when they tell themselves that it is. Consider today's imperceptible-in-principle cosmological "singularities" as a good example of this. Consider also the imperceptible-to-us "many worlds" of contemporary cosmology. Again, none of the "laws of nature" (physics, chemistry, biology, etc.) are directly visible as such; only their effects are perceptible, and they may not even have any effects. They are only conceptual generalizations from our experience of the enduring habits of physical entities, thus only formal but not efficient causes. Laws don't *make* things do what they do; they simply *describe* what they do *en masse.* God, souls, Cartesian minds, fields, singularities, and natural laws explain "things visible" in terms of "things invisible." Neither theologians nor scientists have any hesitation at all about doing that. No clear perceptual line of demarcation separates science from metaphysics, theology, or ethics. Whitehead thought that our separation of science from metaphysics is "purely practical," not theoretical; "Namely, we can agree about science—after due debate—whereas in respect to metaphysics debate has hitherto accentuated disagreement" (*AE* 123). In other words, "science" is just what we tend to agree about; "metaphysics" is what we don't. Even that is too simple to be true.

FIELDS ARE OBJECTIVELY REAL

Though invisible and imperceptible, physical fields are *very real* in the sense that they objectively exist and are not merely subjective, intensional, conceptual, or mathematical concepts or constructs. Whitehead agreed with Plato that being or reality is to be equated with power. Unlike mere concepts and eternal objects, fields have real powers of their own. Most of us are not Berkeleyan idealists or Humean skeptics about the reality of the physical world beyond our own experiences. Mathematics can be applied to physical fields, but critical realists are convinced that field concepts have ontological extensions as well as intra-mental intensions. Reviewing the history of modern science, Einstein noted that physicists insist on the objective reality of fields, but they do not identify them with a plenum of subtle matter, that is, with a "mechanical carrier" called "aether" (146). Whitehead also rejected the "ether" hypothesis (*SMW* 98-99, 115-16, 132) and recognized that "happenings" in electromagnetic fields "are divorced from immediate dependence upon matter" (102).

Neither Whitehead nor Einstein reduced fields to fictional but useful conceptual or mathematical constructs. For Einstein, fields are the most objectively real things of all, and they are manifest in space itself as well as in all observable physical entities. Quite apart from any "material carrier," he wrote, "The field thus becomes an irreducible element of physical description" (150). "The field," he said, "is representative of reality," and we must "conceive of physical reality as a field" (156).

FIELDS ARE PHYSICAL, SPATIALLY EXTENDED

Invisible fields are very *physical* without being directly perceptible to our "external senses." Fields are physical in a very familiar sense: They occupy objective space (or spacetime) and have spatial properties like volume, size, shape, location, movement, etc., even if these are imperceptible, relative, inexact, uncertain, and lack "simple location." Having spatial properties is what most ordinary people, scientists, and philosophers mean by "physical." Physical in this sense is not the same as Whitehead's "physical pole" of actual occasions—their inheritance from the past. As much as we Whiteheadians like to emphasize physical poles, if we are to communicate with most people about the physical, we must also take spatial extension very seriously and treat it as an essential or defining aspect of everything "physical." To the extent that past thoughts influence present and future thoughts, even non-spatial Cartesian minds had physical poles (i.e., they inherited from the past, unless God recreates everything every instant, as Descartes once suggested), but we must somehow account better for the "physical" part of "psycho/physical." Merely having a physical pole (inheriting from the past) will not suffice.

Spatiality as well as temporality is required for "physical," and fields have it. All spatiality requires quantified temporal durations, and all such durations require spatiality. The space that defines the physical for us is not the absolute space of Newtonian physics, characterized by Whitehead as allowing for bits "of matter occupying this region at this durationless instant" (*MT* 146), and where spatially extended matter or physicality is internally vacuous and lacking in experience, activity, purposes, values, and internal process. In pre-quantum/relativity physics, "there is no intrinsic reality" (*SMW* 155) and "Nature is a dull affair, soundless, scentless, colourless, merely the hurrying of material, endlessly, meaninglessly" (54). In contrast, the spatiality of soul-fields is the much richer and very different space of quantum and relativity physics (*SMW*, Chs. VII, VIII) where every indefinite spatial region takes account by degrees of some if not all the others, where space and time are so united that nothing retains all of its spatial qualities in infinitesimally brief durationless instants, and where all actualities exemplify durations and internal feelings, experiences, creativity, values, valuations, and processes (*SMW* 49-55). Traditionally, "matter" was, by definition, spatially extended particulate non-relational stuff (*SMW* 144-45). It is really true even now that "All bodies (particles and their composites) are extended," even though neither bodies nor minds are Cartesian substances. Today "matter" is equated with "energy" or "sheer activity" (*MT* 137-38, *SMW* 35, 101-02,). The concept of the "physical" is now stretched beyond particles to cover waves that are not waving anything particulate, unlike ocean waves that are waving water. "Physical" now applies to spatially extended non-particulate stuff (waves, fields, and space itself). Yet, their "physical" essence is still spatial extension, or better yet, spatiotemporal extension. Einstein and Whitehead both held also that temporal extension or duration is an inseparable part of the essence of physicality, for space and time are inseparable. Although he rejected particulate aether, Einstein was willing to use this word to refer to his own radically new view that space itself has physical properties of its own. Whitehead also willingly spoke of "the ether of events" (*IS* 133).

Space itself, we now know, is something physical, the all-embracing physical field, and it has its own measurable properties and powers. It is not a vacuous void. Particles and waves are nothing more than somewhat indefinite, spatial, quantumized, durational, relational, temporalized energy concentrations. Although physical fields like gravitation and electromagnetism extend through all of spacetime, they are much more concentrated and powerful in some places than in others, more so in a planet than in a grain of sand, more so in a magnet than in an ordinary chunk of iron. Psychophysical fields are also much more intensely concentrated in and around the brains and brain-waves of human beings and the great apes than in jellyfish and amoebas.

FIELDS ENDURE

Physical fields *endure*, but they can be created and destroyed. Magnets, for example, can be manufactured and obliterated, but they have a unity and power of their own. They also endure beyond the particular momentary pulsations of their subordinate electromagnetic happenings, though not beyond all of them taken together. Fields do not endure forever, but they last much longer than their particular ingredients—the events or effects within them. In these respects, they resemble and indeed are the process counterparts of philosophical "substances," as Bracken indicated. Yet, unlike substances, they do not have a self-sufficient and completely independent, non-relational, and unchanging mode of existence; and they can be affected by others. If human souls are field-like, they are by nature very real and relatively enduring unified entities, agents, and patients. They are not self-sufficient or completely independent and unchanging, and when all particulars within them die, they die. Brian G. Henning rightly objects to the complete self-sufficiency, independence, and immutability of traditional substances (83-85, 89), and I completely agree. One of the most important differences between souls as fields and Cartesian mental substances is that soul-fields are spatially extended, whereas Cartesian mental substances were said to be completely "immaterial"; that is, they have no spatial properties at all. Yet, process philosophy can still affirm that ontologically enduring soul-fields are *like* traditional substances in their relative or relational reality, unity, endurance, and agency.

FIELDS ARE CAUSES, AGENTS

Most significant for present purposes, Einstein conceived of fields as enduring wholes that are efficient *causes or agents* (63-65, 98). He wrote that a "magnetic field operates on the piece of iron, so that the latter strives to move towards the magnet" (63), and the gravitational field of the earth "acts on the stone and produces its motion of fall" (64). Whitehead also explicitly recognized the causal effectiveness of fields as such. He wrote of "fields of activity which determine the subsequent events to which they will pass on the objects situated within them" (*CN* 179). The subordinate particles, waves, and events or occasions that occur within fields are causes, but so are the fields themselves. Wholes acts on parts; parts act on other parts and on wholes. Some physical/psychical causation is top-down; some is bottom-up.

Just which particular agent-powers belong to particular fields depends on the kind of field being considered. We discover the particular powers of physical fields through experience, especially those of trained natural scientists. From experience we learn that gravitational fields do one kind of thing, electromagnetic fields do another, and souls do yet another. One of Einstein's greatest frustrations was that he never figured out how to subsume both gravity and electromagnetism under a single field concept, a "Unified Field Theory," and no one since Einstein has succeeded in doing this. No current Unified Field Theories include psychophysical souls, but until they do, they fall short of complete success and unification.

AN EXPANDED CONCEPT OF SOULS AS FIELDS

Now, if Whiteheadians are to follow Bracken in conceiving of enduring human souls as fields, here are a few basic things that we must say about them, some of which clearly go beyond Bracken.

SOULS ARE INVISIBLE, IMPERCEPTIBLE, SELF-PERCEPTIBLE

Enduring human (and animal) souls as such are *invisible and imperceptible* to our external senses, that is, to "perception in the mode of presentational immediacy," as Whitehead would say. They are nevertheless *self-perceptible* in the internal introspective mode of "causal efficacy" or "non-sensuous perception" (*PR* 168-83, 253; *AI* 180-84). As it was in Whitehead's day, the dominant view about natural science today is still that scientific statements are those verifiable or falsifiable by experiences, where "experiences" mean only those of the "external senses," or perceptions in the mode of presentational immediacy. Whiteheadians obviously have a much broader understanding of both "experience" and "science," one that is much more in line with what scientists actually do and say. Souls as psychophysical fields are indeed not directly perceptible to our external senses, but using powerful brain scanning devices, we can now see their most immediate conditions and effects.

SOULS ARE OBJECTIVELY REAL, POTENT

Souls are very *real* in the sense that they have *power* or agency. Being is power. Enduring souls as agents are just as "really real" as ephemeral actual occasions, which are *not* the only "finally real" things in the universe. In his early writings on physical reality, Whitehead agreed with Einstein about the fundamental reality of fields. Recognizing with Einstein the untenability of the material ether hypothesis, Whitehead wrote, "But recently the field itself has come to be conceived as the ultimate fact, and properties of matter have been explained in terms of it" (*IS* 17). If fields themselves are "ultimate facts," then actual occasions are not the only "facts" that count as ultimate or "finally real." Souls as enduring fields are themselves finally real, which means that they are something more than the fleeting actual occasions which they contain and causally constrain or influence. They have properties and powers of their own that their ingredient occasions do not have.

SOULS ARE PHYSICAL AND PSYCHICAL

Souls are *physical* as well as *psychical*. As noted, the essential thing about the physical is that it has spatial extension, which both Einstein and Whitehead thought to be inseparable from temporality. Mere causal inheritance, i.e., having a "physical pole," is not enough. To count as "physical," actual entities and their line of inheritance require spatiality. Whitehead clearly affirmed that *all* actual entities are spatially extended or have "spatial volume" (*PR* 68, 108, 283). "Each final reality," he wrote, "is both physical and mental" (*AI* 190). Process thinkers overcome the dualism of spatially extended bodies versus immaterial minds by insisting that all individual psychic realities have physical (spatial) properties, and all individual physical realities have psychic properties, hence "panexperientialism," as David Griffin calls it. No one was ever able to explain how completely non-spatial Platonic/Cartesian minds could interact with spatially extended bodies. The "field" concept is vitally important here because it affirms the spatiality of otherwise invisible human and animal souls.

Human minds or souls are *not* physical simply because they are *located* in brains (e.g., the pineal gland, according to Descartes) and wider physical environments, or because they *inherit data* from the past. Souls are physical in the sense that they are themselves *spatially extended fields* that surround and pervade human brains. Whitehead thought that human souls were little bitty spatiotemporally extended personal societies that wander about among the empty spaces ("interstices") between our brain cells (*PR* 105-06, 109, 339), but the precise dimensions and whereabouts of soul-fields are definitely up for debate (Cobb, 1965, 82-89; Edwards 1990, 156-66). As Joseph Bracken recognized, applying "field" to enduring societies like human souls is metaphorical (2004, 213), but if souls are spatiotemporally extended realities that pervade human and animal brains, the metaphor is particularly appropriate.

SOULS ARE ENDURING ACTUAL ENTITIES

Unlike actual occasions, souls as fields *endure.* They also have unity, an ongoing *ontological self-identity,* and other properties of their own; but they can also be *created, destroyed, and altered.* All of the biological, physical, social, and relational processes that go into making babies, and then into making persons out of babies, are creative of soul-fields; and improper development, brain diseases, injuries, and degeneration, as well as death daunt, diminish, and destroy them. Enduring soul-fields clearly have contingent *relational* realities. Everyone and everything that have made us into what we are, including our own past decisions, have entered into our very constitution and must be included in a complete answer to "Who am I."

Though obviously contingent, relational, and alterable, soul-fields endure through significant periods of time. Unlike actual occasions, and like God, human souls do not perish every tenth of a second, though when they completely and permanently lose all their content, they cease to exist, at least in this world. Whitehead insisted that actual occasions have duration, a "specious present" (*SMW* 104-05, 124-25). He vaguely suggested that actual occasions on the human level typically endure for about a tenth of a second (*AI* 39, *MT* 181), and, following Charles Hartshorne (1970, 175, 190, 194, 195), most process thinkers today accept this estimate as close enough. For present purposes, this will do. But souls persist much longer than actual occasions. Like the soul of God, our souls do not perish every fraction of a second, but our experiences do because, unlike God, we can't remember them vividly, completely, and constantly.

Whitehead clearly recognized one enduring and processing reality with prolonged self-identity and originative causality, but not composed of or reducible to an extended society of actual occasions, namely, God. He viewed God as a single, everlasting, continuously concresceing actual entity (*PR* 18, 40, 46, 65, 87, 94, 110, 164, 244), so it is really not true for the Whitehead of *Process and Reality* that "Agency belongs exclusively to actual occasions" (31). Unlike the process God of Hartshorne, who is composed of an infinite set of temporally successive actual occasions, Whitehead's God successively processes and experiences the succession of actual occasions in the world without being temporal, that is, without being himself composed of successive actual occasions. The temporal succession of perishing actual occasions is perceived continuously but successively by God, who is a single non-perishing actual entity. Whitehead's God is one, everlasting, constantly and openly concresceing, actual entity who absorbs and never loses the world *as it comes into being in time*. Nothing ever perishes or is lost to God. God constantly and sequentially experiences the succession of events in the world without succeeding himself or perishing as an actual entity. Whitehead wrote, "No thinker thinks twice," and "no subject experiences twice" (*PR* 29). Yet, God does; and so do we as enduring fields. As I suggested several decades ago (Edwards 1975), perhaps human souls (understood now in this work as enduring fields) are analogous to God as a single enduring actual entity—but without God's necessary existence, everlasting endurance, faultless memory, and overall perfection.

He rejected fields for this, as he told me in personal correspondence, but Lewis Ford developed his own account of human selves as enduring single actual entities having "open concrescence," like God's. This means we need not perish ontologically in order to achieve value, unity, and definiteness, or to produce effects beyond ourselves (Ford 291-318). This, I think, is exactly what process thinkers need if they are going to take ethics seriously, and if they are going to be taken seriously as ethicists. Without something like this, process thinkers cannot account adequately for real people as we know them and their worth. The way we actually experience and value ourselves and our personal unity and endurance is much better expressed metaphysically in terms of continuously concresceing relatively enduring fields than as transmitted subjective forms and societies of fleeting actual occasions. Combining Ford with Bracken (despite their possible protests), I propose that souls are unified and relatively enduring fields with open concrescence. *Souls as enduring actual entities make a place within process thought for relative ontological, not just psychological, continuity and self-identity through time.*

SOULS ARE ORIGINATIVE CAUSAL AGENTS

Souls as enduring fields are *causes or agents,* and their agency is not identical with or reducible to the agency of the particular actual occasions that they contain and constrain. Enduring souls can do things that single actual occasions cannot do; they have powers that actual occasions do not have, either singly or in groups. If being is power, enduring souls have a fundamental being or reality of their own that is different from and not reducible to the reality and activity of their actual occasions. Whitehead was wrong in insisting that agency belongs exclusively to individual actual occasions. Agency also belongs to ontologically enduring unique individuals like God and human and animal souls. Soul-agency is creative, originative and is manifest in "self-determined" free choices, attention-power, self-control, etc.

The ontological status or reality of souls has great significance for two concerns of ethics or axiology, first, we are personally responsible or accountable for what we freely choose to do, as next explained; second, persons are ends in themselves, intrinsically good, as explained in the following chapter. I am responsible for my choices; my actual occasions are not; I have intrinsic worth, not just my actual occasions, assuming that they have any worth at all. All of these claims will be further explained and defended.

SOUL FIELDS, AGENCY, AND RESPONSIBILITY

Whiteheadians subscribe to the view that being responsible for what we choose to do, for better or worse, means originating our choices to do such things ourselves as agents, instead of having our choices programmed into us from eternity by God or by causal antecedents in our environment and our own genetic and/or personal history. As Whitehead said,

> In the case of those actualities whose immediate experience is most completely open to us, namely, human beings, the final decision of the immediate subject-superject, constituting the ultimate modification of subjective aim is the foundation of our experience of responsibility, of approbation or disapprobation, of self-approval or of self-reproach, of freedom, of emphasis. (*PR* 47)

Whiteheadians affirm self-creativity and originative personal agency, not theological predestination or secular philosophical determinism. With Whitehead, I am in full agreement that "the actual entity, in a state of process during which it is not fully definite, determines its own ultimate definiteness. This is the whole point of moral responsibility" (*PR* 255); but much remains to be clarified.

One crucial consideration is this. Are only transient actual occasions creative and responsible agents, or are enduring soul-fields as such also creative and responsible agents? To deal with this we must consider whether we experience ourselves doing anything as enduring persons that fleeting actual occasions cannot do, and if they do what we cannot do. If the answer is "Yes," then responsible agency does not belong exclusively with and is not reducible to that of the fleeting actual occasions within our stream of consciousness. The real difference between Whitehead's entities that are "finally real" (actual occasions) and those that are only derivatively or secondarily real (collective enduring societies like human souls) is that for Whitehead himself only the former are responsible agents, not the latter. As Whitehead said, a "society is only efficient through its individual members" (*PR* 91) and "Agency belongs exclusively to actual occasions" (*PR* 31).

But what if enduring human and animal soul-fields are responsible for things and can actually do things and that no tenth-of-a-second occasion, and no merely additive succession of such, can do? In that case, agency belongs not exclusively to actual occasions but to enduring soul-fields as well. It seems to me that inner self-experience in the mode of causal efficacy discloses that *I as an enduring self can do things that my component actual occasions cannot do*, and that *they can do things that I cannot do*. Our powers are not identical, so souls and transient occasions are not identical. I am something more than the sum of my parts in a very fundamental or "finally real" way.

To begin with *what they can do but I cannot,* every actual occasion is a "creative synthesis" a "concrescence," that pulls together data and ideals from the past and from God, unifies them into a tenth-of-a-second or so unity, definiteness, and completeness, then perishes. As a "superject," it then passes on its achievements to what comes next. But if I ask, "Is this something that I do every tenth of a second?" the answer is clearly, "No." Time marches on, including my subjectively experienced time, no matter what I try to do, or do not try to do. I do not actively, deliberately, intentionally, and effortfully do or decide *anything* in a tenth of a second, even if my actual occasions do. Their fleeting initial aims and choices among them are not my actual aims and choices. The creativity of any single occasion or any set of such fleeting occasions within my own soul-field or stream of consciousness is not *my* creativity. Their creative synthesis is not my creative synthesis.

When awake, I concresce or pull and hold things together extensively and whole-istically over spans of time. My ingredient soul-field occasions blow their concrescence in a tenth of a second, and I cannot make them do it, or stop them, or speed them up, or slow them down. The creative synthesizing or concresceing of the occasions within my soul-field just *happens to me.* This is not something that *I do.* Concrescence, what Hartshorne called "creative synthesis" just happens, whether I try, or care, or not. I cannot start it. I cannot stop it. I am as passive with respect to temporal concrescence as with respect to receiving sensations from external objects. The actual occasions within my soul-field definitely do things that I do not do, and they have powers that I do not have. They concresce, expend their power, then perish in a tenth of a second. I do not. From an enduring-self perspective, the relentless concrescence of transient actual occasions within my stream of consciousness is an expression of the universe's creativity, but not of my own personal creativity.

What can *I do that my occasions cannot do?* I as an enduring soul-field can do things and have powers that my ingredient actual occasions cannot do and do not have, so I am more than the mere sum of my transient parts. I have an overall ontological continuity and self-identity. I have an inclusive and comprehensive continuing perspective on, and can give ongoing and inclusive directives and purposes to, the fleeting occasions within my stream of soul-consciousness. No merely additive sequence of occasions could do this, for no one of them, and no set of them, so comprehends, includes, and directs the whole. Yet, I do. A tenth of a second actual occasion might objectify itself within the next tenth and pass along its own tiny aims, but I do not see how it could grasp and pass along a set of *enduring* intentions, objectives, thoughts, or actions to anything—but I can. I as a personal enduring field of consciousness function as an overall inclusive field-force who remembers, anticipates, directs, controls, and acts far beyond the present moment. As a unique personal conscious soul-field, I function as a relatively enduring organic whole that far transcends the functioning of the sum of my transient temporal parts.

The basic logic here is this. If a single actual occasion does not have a given property, P, and if two or many more successive members of a set or nexus, S (for soul), do not have P, then S does not and could not have P, if it is merely the sum of its members. But suppose that S has property P anyway. Then S is a distinctive organic whole with emergent properties of its own not possessed by any of its members. This S as a whole is more than an additive sequence, more than the sum of its transient parts.

Whitehead himself came very close to seeing this when he explained why Hume's "association of ideas" cannot account for what is going on when someone thinks or "enunciates" the phrase "United Fruit Company."

> In his experience the relation of the latter to the earlier parts of this phrase is entirely the same as that described above for the phrase 'United States'. In this latter example it is to be noted that

while association would have led him to 'States', the fact of the energizing of the immediate past compelled him to conjoin 'Fruit' in the immediacy of the present. He uttered the word 'United' with the non-sensuous anticipation of an immediate future with the sensum 'Fruit', and he then uttered the word 'Fruit' with the non-sensuous perception of the immediate past with the sensum 'United." . . . The final occasion of his experience which drove his body to the utterances of the sound 'Company' is only explicable by his concerns with the earlier occasions with their subjective forms of intention to procure the utterance of the complete phrase. Also in so far as there was consciousness, there was direct observation of the past with its intention finding its completion on the present fact. This is an instance of direct intuitive observation which is incapable of reduction to the sensationist formula. (*AI* 182-183)

Whitehead's primary purpose here was to give a clear example of internal intuitive experience, observation, and non-sensuous introspective perception in the mode of causal efficacy, one not reducible to the presentational immediacy of sensations derived from the so-called "external senses." However, his example illustrates much more than this. It shows that many things that we think, intend, and do take much more time than a tenth of a second, and that some sort of lasting entity exercises a holistic or gestalt comprehension of and control over spans of transient occasions. It shows that the fleeting intentions (subjective aims and forms) of many past transient occasions have an overall organic and ontological unity and causality that is far more than the merely additive unity and causality of the transient successive occasions themselves. It shows that the enduring soul functions as a unitary whole. It shows that an enduring soul-field, and not just its fleeting actual occasions, is efficient in, as, and for itself, and that agency belongs to it and not exclusively to its ingredient actual occasions. A tenth of a second occasion might intend and bring about part of the "U," but I comprehensively intend, control, and bring about the whole—"United Fruit Company." I can think a whole thought, comprehend a whole paragraph, write a whole book. Whitehead was simply mistaken when he wrote, "The soul is nothing else than the succession of my occasions of experience, extending from birth to the present moment" (*MT* 163).

Human soul-level self-control, deliberation, decision-making, long range planning and purposing, sustained effort-making, prolonged self-evaluation, and ongoing self-respect and self-valuation, well illustrate the holistic self-identity, agency, and ontological endurance of overall soul-fields as such. No one actual occasion, or any merely additive succession of them, has these properties, but I do. If every occasion lacks them, then the whole could not have them if it is merely their sum. Only wholes that are greater than the sum of their parts can have properties and powers not possessed by them.

I do not experience myself as making creative free-will decisions every tenth of a second. Making soul-level choices takes much more time, and I make choices only occasionally, not ten times a second. Extended deliberation and prolonged desires, often conflicting and none strongest until I decide, precede and accompany my choices. None of this is completely contained in, controlled by, or passed along through any particular tenth of a second, or any set or nexus of such, where all individual members lack them. I can willfully initiate and terminate sustained efforts of thinking, feeling, and doing; but the starting and stopping of actual occasions is inevitable and beyond my control. I do not respect or value myself or anyone else in or as a tenth of a second. Yet evaluations of my enduring self and others are integral aspects of who I am, and of what ethics requires of us. I doubt that any of us has ever valued a single actual occasion within our own or anyone's stream of consciousness. A large sum of non-valued occasions never adds up to a positive self-valuation that is more than the sum of such non-valuations. The things that we value about ourselves and others are much more enduring. We treasure our pasts, and we make long range plans for our futures—as if these were integral to our very constitution. And they are.

It is perhaps surprising that Whitehead himself did not see a connection between his own concept of "organism" and that of "field." Both are concepts of enduring wholes that causally structure and affect their transient parts, while also being affected by them. Many thanks to Bracken for finally getting it! Whitehead knew of, and we are now even more familiar with, many field-like efficacious enduring organic realities that preside over and exert causal influence over vast sets of ephemeral temporal occurrences. A very good example of this is the development of a human embryo from a single cell into a complex living organism. At conception, and through several stages of cell division, an embryo is composed of sets of stem cells having *identical* properties internally. It is only after subsets of these cells *position* themselves spatially in relation to other subsets of cells that they start to differentiate into distinctive organs in particular places within the embryo complex. Being internally identical up to this point, how do these cells know when and where to differentiate themselves into what externally? Why don't they just proliferate indefinitely as undifferentiated identical stem cells? All still have exactly the same set of genes after they differentiate into unique organs and structures, so what makes them differentiate? Some enduring master psychophysical bio-field must be presiding over and directing the process. So it is with the human soul and its ingredient occasions. As David Griffin indicated, "The characteristic forms taken up by molecules, crystals, cells, tissues, organs, and organisms are shaped and maintained by specific fields called *morphogenetic fields*" (1988, 81), and "For more than 50 years, embryologists and developmental biologists have used this term [fields] to refer to the unknown structuring and organizing factors that enable animals and plants to develop from eggs, through various embryonic stages into their characteristic adult forms" (82).

Enduring master psychophysical bio-fields may exist far beyond human beings and animals, and even far beyond individuals having a central nervous system. In his immensely important 2005 book, *The Ethics of Creativity,* Brian G. Henning follows Frederick Ferré in speculating, "Some plants may be sufficiently complex to support a form of personal society that provides some degree of central coordination" (163). The psychophysical bio-field or morphogenetic field concept may be a way to further expand the significant insight that even some plants may have primitive souls. I am concerned about the *proper limits* for applying field concepts, but *I really do not know what they are.* Looking and acting as a unit seems highly relevant. Quantum era science discloses that we really do live in a spooky universe, but we definitely do not want to return to a primitive animism that assigns a soul-field to every stick, rock, ecosystem, or planet that we run across. We also do not want to limit fields too severely. Much work remains to be done here.

We mature human beings experience ourselves as being responsible for (knowingly being the originative cause of) our past decisions, some from long ago. This is because we know that we made them, not some actual occasion ancestor that perished in the distant past. We feel guilt for the bad ones and some degree of pride and satisfaction for the good ones. Explaining this has been a real challenge for process thinkers. How can I as a perishing present actual occasion, or a closely affiliated set of such, feel responsible for decisions made by past occasions that perished long ago, even if they are within my personal cone of causation or line of inheritance?

Hartshorne (1970, xix-xx, 190-204) argued that being presently concerned for my own distant future is truly altruistic because my future actual occasions are very different, distinct, and distant from those now present. Well, the same considerations apply retrospectively to responsibility for past decisions. How can I be responsible now for distant past decisions made by very different and distinct transient occasions, even if they were in my own past history, but they aren't me now? The standard Whiteheadian answer is that to a significant degree we have the same personality today that we had back then; that is, we still have or are the same feelings, interests, desires, emotions, beliefs, dispositions, behaviors, and "subjective forms." Psychological continuity alone accounts for personal responsibility, Whitehead and Hartshorne thought. This means, I am responsible for the terrible thing that I did to someone years ago because I still have the same immoral and antisocial motives, beliefs, and dispositions I had years ago. Up to some point, this "continuity of subjective forms" explanation seems to work, but *not if I have changed significantly*. This standard Whiteheadian position logically implies that if I am a "new-born" or "second-born" soul and do *not* have the same immoral desires and personality traits that I had back then, then I am *not* responsible because *I* didn't do it! It just wasn't *me!*

The trouble is, so many people, myself included, do feel responsible and repentant for the terrible things we did to someone else, to some animal, to some living thing, years ago, even though we are no longer by any means the immorally disposed persons we were back then. Sameness of subjective forms or psychological continuity will not explain this sense of responsibility because there is no sameness. Psychologically, we have become different persons, so we should feel no responsibility at all, if Whitehead and Hartshorne are right. Yet, we do; and reflecting on standard process metaphysics won't make this go away.

Placing an evil deed within our past cone of causation will not explain our profound sense of responsibility even after we have really changed, *unless* metaphysically we are somehow the same persons we were back then, unless something significant about us then and now is ontologically continuous and relatively self-identical. Enduring selves or soul-fields adequately account for our ontological continuity and responsibility, but subjective continuity (lacking, by hypothesis in these cases), and merely falling within a single line of inheritance, do not. As enduring souls, we are something more than the mere sum and motivational sameness of our successive past and present actual occasions. Whitehead's relatively sparse statements about morality and our human obligations and responsibilities all presuppose the fundamental reality and agency of enduring souls, but he never showed us how to get this from his metaphysics of actual occasions as the only full realities and actual agents.

SOULS AND COMPLETE HUMAN BEINGS

My total reality is a synthesis of permanence and change, soul and body, and so is my total worth. If I am both my own enduring embodied psychophysical soul-field *and* all of its contents, past, present, and potentially future, this yields a very rich process answer to "Who am I?" *I am the unified and self-integrated totality of all my ontological, qualitative, and relational structures, properties, experiences, and activities, both transient and more enduring.* I am my enduring ontological self plus every experience I have ever had, every thought, formality, or belief I have ever entertained, every feeling, emotion, desire, pleasure, pain, or mood I have ever felt, every deed I have ever done, every mere "thing" or macroscopic physical object I have ever perceived, and every person, animal, or living thing who has ever entered into or touched my life in any way. My total reality exemplifies both permanence and change, both ontological continuity and profound relationality.

We are unfinished enduring souls, constantly adding relational and occasional properties. New properties not always present are nevertheless not accidental or unessential aspects of *our integrated total property self-inventories*. Together with our enduring soul-fields, all added properties are fully constitutive of our very reality, of who we are, of our total being and becoming. Without many qualifications we cannot "hate the sin but love the sinner" because the sinner is his or her sinful dispositions, decisions, and deeds, plus a lot of other very good stuff. Both homosexuals and heterosexuals are their sexualities, and we cannot affirm them without affirming their sexuality, for that is integral to who they are.

We are the integrated but unfinished and constantly increasing holistic totalities of our soul-fields and all of our properties and relations. All are constitutive of our total intrinsic reality and worth as unique concrete individual subjects of value and evaluation. This is more carefully explained in the following chapter. Thus, we are incalculably rich in intrinsic-good-making properties. Sadly, most of who we really are is lost to our feeble memories, but not to God's flawless memory. Only God knows who we really are. Through God's memory, everything is granted objective immortality. If we have any kind of immortality, objective or subjective, it is solely by the grace and power of God, not by our own strength or merit.

Self-enrichment through time happens to every relatively enduring soul or self. Our realities as enduring but still becoming conscious selves are incredibly full and fulfilled in good-making properties, but our bad-making properties are also there within us. The quantity of our inherent qualities and constitutive relations, many relatively enduring, is practically incalculable, though not infinite. Every positive thought, feeling, and action we have ever had or performed is integral to our very constitution and goodness (or badness). In process thought, our being involves our becoming, and we are unfinished, unified, integrated, conscious realities or totalities. Time is constantly adding new experiences, activities, relations, and properties, as Whitehead well understood (*AI* 205-06). Our negative properties, our bad-making qualities and relations, the evils within us, are equally constitutive of our being and becoming. Most theologians would insist that our negativities cannot be ignored in a comprehensive view of human souls.

Having reached a process understanding of the human self or soul, we have not yet arrived at the total human being, the "whole man" (or woman). Our self or soul is the dominant personally ordered society of actual occasions within our human bodies, or better yet, our embodied, dominant, enduring psychophysical field and its contents. As Whitehead insisted, dominant psychophysical realities require the support of, and only exist within, even wider psychophysical societies of structures, organs, cells, and temporal occasions (*AI* 189, 205; *MT* 159-61). Human souls are always embodied, and the human body is an absolutely essential part of every total human being. When parts of our brains do not work, our souls do not work accordingly. Not only are personal souls psychical, they are also *physical, because they are spatially extended.* They necessarily exist within extended human bodies and require them as support systems. As total human beings, we are the dominant enduring actual entities within our bodies, plus our bodies themselves, which are integral aspects of who we are. Our souls and bodies are one.

This is the really important way in which postmodern process thought avoids the radical mind/body dualism of Cartesian and much post-Cartesian (i.e., "modern") philosophy. A complete human being is both body and soul, neither of which is radically different in kind or in psychophysical properties from the other. I as a human being am both my body and my soul—psychophysical throughout. The human body is composed of experiencing cells, differentiated into structures and organs—psychophysical throughout. These cells are lesser enduring psychophysical entities that both support and feed information to one another and into the dominant personal enduring soul. The cells of our bodies provide experiences and amplify feelings for our souls. One of Whitehead's most interesting expressions of what he called "the unity of 'body and mind'" in a complete human person is, "No one ever says, Here am I, and I have brought my body with me" (*MT* 114; compare 205 and *AI* 189, 205). Souls cannot exist or experience in the absence of a wider supportive psychophysical environment. This has great significance for the theological dispute over whether disembodied souls survive after death, or whether such survival requires something like the resurrection of a transformed body, though that is beyond the scope of this discussion. Bracken's theory of souls as fields has clear and important implications for issues of survival after death. Soul-fields require total-embodied-person-fields.

2.

INTRINSIC VALUES AND UNIQUE INDIVIDUALS

What kind of *value* do persons and animals with enduring souls have? One of the most fundamental concepts of ethics is that of "intrinsic value" or "intrinsically good." By widespread agreement, this means being valuable or desirable to, in, and for itself, or being an end in itself (Henning 57-60). Brian Henning and other interpreters of Whitehead's ethics do much more with the concept of "intrinsic value" than Whitehead himself. Whitehead had no general definition of "good" to offer, but he did formulate his own understanding of "intrinsically good," and this is a good place to begin, even if more is required.

INTRINSICALLY VALUABLE ACTUAL ENTITIES

When all is said and done, we will find that the essential good-making properties of intrinsically good realities or actual entities are 1. Self-significance, 2. Consciousness, 3. Endurance, 4. Individuality, and 5. Uniqueness. Whitehead himself emphasized self-significance, but these additional essential good-making properties of intrinsically good entities are either implicit within or presupposed by self-significance, and it is best to make them explicit from the outset.

SELF-SIGNIFICANCE: VALUATION OF SELF OR BY SELF?

Discussions of intrinsic goodness are very hard but not impossible to find in Whitehead's own writings. Whitehead was no systematic ethicist or axiologist. In *Science and the Modern World* he said, "An actual event is an achievement for its own sake" (104), and "The element of value, of being valuable, of having value, of being an end in itself, of being something which is for its own sake, must not be omitted in any account of an event as the most concrete actual something. 'Value' is the word I use for the intrinsic reality of an event" (9). Some of his best relevant remarks are in *Modes of Thought*.

> At the base of our existence is the sense of "worth." Now worth essentially presupposes that which is worthy . . . It is the sense of existence for its own sake, of existence which is its own justification, of existence with its own character. (109)

> A dead nature aims at nothing. It is the essence of life that it exists for its own sake, as the intrinsic reaping of value. (135)

> The basis of democracy is the common fact of value experience, as constituting the essential nature of each pulsation of actuality. Everything has some value for itself, for others, and for the whole. (111)

> The phrase "intrinsic importance" means "importance for itself." (118)

> The essence of power is the drive towards aesthetic worth for its own sake. All power is a derivative from this fact of composition attaining worth for itself. (119)

In many discussions, Whitehead seemed to equate "intrinsic worth" with "self-enjoyment" (AI 219; MT 150-55), or perhaps with "significance for itself" understood to mean that it "functions with respect to its own determination" (PR 25). Since "importance" for Whitehead was a synonym for "good" or "value," "importance for itself" means "value for itself." But what do these phrases mean, especially the "self" or "itself" parts? And does the "for" mean "by" or "to"? Do Whitehead's phrases mean that every intrinsically valuable being is constantly directly aware of itself, distinguishes itself from what is not itself, focuses its attention directly on itself, enjoys or takes pleasure in itself, deliberately creates itself, or attaches some kind of positive value to itself as well as to other things? Is something as complex as such self-awareness, self-enjoyment, self-creation, and self-valuation present in every actual occasion, no matter how simple? Just how far down into the great chain of becoming do these "self" properties go? Do they clearly and constantly apply to us human beings, to all animals, perhaps to some plants and cells? Do they go even deeper into molecules, atoms, and subatomic particles and waves?

So understood, do these properties apply *constantly* even to us human beings? This is very doubtful. The presence and necessity of self-awareness in human beings has been greatly exaggerated. On one interpretation, Immanuel Kant believed that the thought of "I" accompanies or is constantly present in all human experience and judgments. It is often said that the difference between us and the other animals is that we are self-aware or self-conscious whereas they are merely aware or conscious. One crucial concern here is *constancy*. Whitehead was keenly aware that consciousness is only intermittent and not constant in human life. It is present only when we are not asleep or "knocked out," but are we always keenly self-aware when we are awake? This is very doubtful.

On another interpretation, Kant believed that the thought of "I" is *capable* of being present in all human experience and judgments, not constantly present, but occasionally. To draw a parallel, are Whitehead's "self-significance" or "self-enjoyment" constantly present in every actual occasion, or are they present only occasionally within the overall streams of consciousness of enduring souls? Is self-awareness really a constant factor in human consciousness, or in animal consciousness, and below?

Without it, how could there be any self-significance or self-enjoyment?

Intellectuals and egotists tend greatly to overestimate the degree to which "self" is a direct object of human awareness. David Hume insisted that we are never aware of it. Without lapsing into Humean skepticism, we must acknowledge that some of the most wonderful moments of our lives are so completely and passionately focused on *valuing other things* that we have no thought or immediate awareness of *self* at all. Moments of intense and passionate creativity in art, music, writing, and philosophy must be so described, also moments of intense and passionate love, as well as ecstatic moments of absorption into the sublime, whether that of nature or of God. In peak experiences, self awareness is lost, and the self is completely absorbed in valuing another. During the very best times of our lives, we are not thinking "I," or valuing, enjoying, or even aware of self at all. Rather, we are valuing, enjoying, completely absorbed in, and intensely aware of other things, other intentional value-objects.

Prepositions can be tricky. Whitehead's "significance *for* self" could mean "valuation *of* self," or "valuation *by* self." His "self-enjoyment" could mean "enjoyment *of* self" or "enjoyment *by* self." Self awareness and self valuation are only intermittent. *Only valuation by self is a constant of consciousness.* If these expressions partly define intrinsic worth—being an end in itself, being valuable for its own sake—then only evaluation as such, not valuation of self, is universal in all conscious human occasions. With some plausibility, only evaluation as such, or evaluation *by self,* is widespread below the human level. Whitehead explained, "Actuality is the self-enjoyment of importance. But this self-enjoyment has the character of the self-enjoyment of others melting into the enjoyment of the one self" (*MT* 117-18). By "others" he meant actual occasions in our own recent past, not other people or animals, but there is no reason why this could not be extended to other souls or objects of value. Though probably not Whitehead's view, and definitely not my view, Charles Hartshorne subscribed to the peculiar theory that all introspection is really only retrospection on immediately past occasions within our stream of consciousness (1970, 109). If so, no actual occasions have any immediate awareness or enjoyment of themselves at all, and all intrinsically valuable entities value only others.

Hereafter, to avoid cumbersome qualifications, we will usually speak of *valuing self or others* or perhaps just *valuation*. Human beings are only intermittently rational, conscious, self-aware, self-valuing, and other-valuing; but we are *constantly valuing something* in all our waking moments. Consciousness or awareness is evaluation. Intrinsically valuable entities are those that value *something,* but not necessarily themselves, and not constantly themselves.

Also, evaluation as such is never "for its own sake;" it is always for the sake of some conscious individual, and it exists only within conscious individuals. The concept of "valuation" will be examined more carefully in Chapter Four, but note for now that it can be either positive or negative. In Whitehead's words, valuation can be either "adversion" or "aversion."

To be sure, self-awareness and self-valuation are important. They have great value. They are good-making properties of at least some experiencing individuals some of the time. They must be very primitive if present at atomic and sub-atomic levels, but they can also become much more advanced or complex by degrees. The most refined degrees are exemplified by those human and non-human animals that can pass the mirror test for self-recognition. This test is much used today to determine if some animals are self-conscious and have a "self-concept." Non-human animals like the great apes and dolphins can pass this test, but intermittent lesser self-awareness and self-valuation surely belongs to those less complex animals who cannot recognize their images in mirrors.

As someone pointed out, tigers, who cannot recognize their own mirror image, nevertheless do not eat their own paws when consuming their prey! Occasionally, they are immediately aware of who, what, and where they are, what they are experiencing and doing, where their own bodies end, and where the rest of the world begins. They are attuned to what supports and what threatens themselves. On some primitive level, and by degrees, all self-valuing or significant-to-self individuals must periodically be aware of themselves somehow. Just how far this goes into the depths of *the great chain of becoming,* I do not claim to know. We process thinkers hope that "finding *something* significant" goes all the way to the bottom, even if "find *self* significant" does not.

CONSCIOUSNESS

If self or other valuation exists at cellular and sub-cellular levels of becoming, how much of it is conscious and how much is unconscious? Hartmanian formal axiology can be enriched by what process thinkers say about panexperientialism and the intrinsic goodness of animals and the rest of the sub-human world, but that depends on whether experiencing and valuing in most of the non-human world is or is not totally unconscious, and what that means.

Clearly, much human experiencing and valuing is unconscious, and we should be very thankful that our brains and bodies do so much of our unconscious or subconscious work for us. But what exactly is *our* unconsciousness? What is unconscious to our souls may be only low-grade consciousness in our bodily cells, especially our brain cells. My unconsciousness is their consciousness! Lewis Ford suggested this to me in email correspondence some time ago, and I suspect that he is right. If cells and their molecules and atoms really are *totally* unconscious, it is hard to see how they could have any intrinsic worth at all, or what "experiencing," "self-significance," or "valuing self or others" could mean when applied to them. Whitehead occasionally contrasted consciousness with more primitive feelings (*PR* 241-43), but don't or can't feelings involve degrees of consciousness? Would entities having only totally unconscious feelings have any intrinsic worth? Who cares about enjoyment if there is no awareness of it? Who cares about pain as long as it is totally unconscious? Would anything matter at all to totally unconscious beings?

Whitehead held that no actualities are "vacuous," that all actualities experience, process creatively, and have value (*RM* 100). Indeed "Everything has some value for itself, for others, and for the whole" (*MT* 111), and "The phrase 'intrinsic importance' means 'importance for itself'" (118). But could all actualities, including cells, molecules, atoms, electrons, protons, etc., have intrinsic value, or find themselves or others to be important, without some degree of consciousness? Consciousness is inherently intentional; it has an object, and that object is its value-object or object valued. This might be self or another, and the other could belong to any grade of reality or dimension of value, intrinsic, extrinsic, or systemic. It could be anywhere in time, past, present, or future. It could be a mere possibility or a concrete actuality. It could be attractive or repulsive. Given our analysis this far, intrinsically valuable entities must be unique individuals with some capacity for valuing self or something, but does "totally unconscious valuing of self or something" (where not even brain cells have valuational awareness) make any sense? Should we not make "consciousness" another defining property of "intrinsic worth? This depends largely on what "consciousness" means.

Most of us are very uncertain about how to define it, but we know very well from experience what *consciousness* is. As Whitehead recognized, "Consciousness, like everything else, is in a sense indefinable. It is just itself and must be experienced" (*AI* 269). We experience consciousness every time we wake up from a good night's sleep, and we lose it nightly or whenever we go to sleep. We know that through it we are aware of many things and that we can internally take account of, respond to, and attach significance or value both to our external environment and to our internal awareness. An awareness resembling consciousness is present in our dreams. We know that consciousness is embodied, that it is intimately related to the functioning of our brains and the rest of our bodies. We really do not know how, but there are many theories about this—like the embodied soul-field theory developed earlier. Some mind/body theories are more plausible than others, but none are absolutely definitive. We know experientially that our own consciousness is very real and causally effective. Consciousness partly accounts for our intrinsic goodness. Self-valuation or self-enjoyment make no sense without it.

When awake, we can be aware of our sensations, of what is present in and happening within our environment, and we can also be aware of ourselves, of what is present to and going on within our own bodies and souls. We can be aware of what Whitehead called "the witness of the body" (*PR* 81, 62-63, 170, 311-13). We can also be immediately and directly aware of our own thoughts, feelings, aims, purposes, choices, and actions, and of their transience and temporality. Further, we are concerned about our enduring selves as well as our own passing thoughts, feelings, purposes, choices, and actions. Such things matter greatly to us. By nature, we are self-concerned, self-interested, and value ourselves and others. We anticipate and care about our own pasts and futures, what we were, and what we will think, feel, experience, choose, and do tomorrow and later. We also care about these things in others. We plan ahead, though some of us do this better and further than others. Most of us have long-range plans of life, though these vary in specificity and range. We are valuable to, for, and in ourselves partly because we are directly and consciously aware of and concerned about ourselves and/or others. Our enjoyment of self and not-self is conscious.

So we know what consciousness is when we experience it, but how should we define it? Whitehead thought that consciousness involves *an awareness and positive or negative evaluation* of contrasts, definiteness, affirmations, and negations (*PR* 243, 267, 273-74). Consciousness involves an internal awareness of the difference between p and not p, between what is, what is not, and what might be. What could that mean when applied to entities at the lower end of the great chain of becoming? Perhaps actual occasions within atoms and electrons have it in their own exceedingly minute way, but I do not claim to know for sure.

Electrons seem to be sensitive, responsive, and excited when new quanta of energy are added to them—otherwise not. They know when they are and are not faced with two slits to have to go through. (They can't go through three.) Do all actual occasions (at any level) have at least a dim consciousness of the difference between p and not p? Surely they must, given Whitehead's analysis of "concrescence," because every concresceing actual occasion knows what data it has and has not (negative prehensions) inherited from its immediate past, and it must decide which of the multiple ideals or subjective aims inherited from God or its earlier self to affirm—or not. Even in the lowest grade actual occasions, valuing self or another seems quite impossible and downright unintelligible without some dim or vague consciousness of what is and what is not self or other. Distinguishing p from not p is the defining characteristic of consciousness, according to Whitehead, but given his analysis of "concrescence," every actual occasion makes such distinctions. So we will indeed add "consciousness" to the list of defining traits of intrinsically good actualities, even if it is exceedingly low-grade and simple, as it must surely be in the occasions of atomic and sub-atomic particles. Without it, they could have no intrinsic worth (which they may not have), but we will assume with Whitehead that they do.

ENDURANCE

Do and should we regard persons (or non-human subjects) in the sense of *enduring* self-or-other valuing individuals as intrinsically good, as valuable for their own sake, as ends in themselves? Or do only the fleeting actual occasions within our streams of consciousness have intrinsic worth? Or both?

When we value persons as ends, we actually value them holistically, not occasion by occasion. When we truly love another person, we love *all their space, all their time, and all their good-making properties*, including those that make them unique and those that endure. We never, if ever, value single actual occasions. So, what is the value of *enduring* individual persons, according to process thought? To answer, we must return to our original problem, "What is an individual person?" and to a central affirmation of Hartmanian axiology, "Unique individual persons are intrinsically good."

Whitehead himself emphasized "the importance of the individual" (*AI* 292) and "the intrinsic importance of an experience," which means "importance for itself" (*MT* 118). However, we cannot infer from "an experience" that he thought that *enduring unique persons who have experiences* are either important or intrinsically good. As noted, Whitehead held that the only real individuals and agents are momentary temporal occasions, enduring for only fractions of a second (*AI* 177, 186). Whitehead clearly affirmed importance and intrinsic worth for these, but did he do so clearly enough for persons in the ordinary sense of enduring persons existing from birth to death in a more lasting, holistic, and inclusive sense? He affirmed that actual occasions have importance, intrinsic worth, and exist for their own sake; but do I, do other people as enduring wholes, have intrinsic worth? This is not a question about the self of the fleeting moment. It is about something much more durable and inclusive. In *Modes of Thought,* Whitehead clearly tied individual immediacy of self-enjoyment, the defining property of intrinsic worth, only to fleeting occasions of experience (150-51), from which it follows that only they, but not enduring souls, have intrinsic worth.

John Cobb wrote, "From a Whiteheadian perspective, the absence of any substantial identity through time does not necessarily lead to disparaging an emphasis on personal identity. We do inherit most of what we are in each moment from antecedent moments of personal experience. . . There can, therefore, be spiritualities based on enduring personal existence in distinction from those that focus on momentary existence" (Cobb, Epperly, Nancarrow, 27). My complaint is not that process thinkers entirely neglect total or enduring selfhood in favor of momentary selfhood, only that this needs deeper analysis, greater emphasis, and a process metaphysics of soul-fields that clearly and unambiguously allows for enduring ontological selfhood, agency, and intrinsic worth.

Process thought could be deepened by recognizing that we do in fact identify with our unified total enduring selves in many morally and spiritually significant ways, whereas we never, if ever, consciously identify ourselves with our momentary psychic pulsations. Expressed axiologically, after careful consideration, we do intrinsically value ourselves as unique enduring subjects as ends. As inclusive souls, we are valuable for our own sakes. In our moral moments, we also evaluate other people that way, though the scope of our intrinsic concern for others may be pathetically limited. Moral and spiritual growth consists largely in expanding the scope or range of our intrinsic concern for ourselves and other unique *enduring* individualities.

Not only do we value our unified *enduring selves,* we also highly value and identify ourselves with many *enduring states of character,* dispositions, or virtues like prudence, courage, temperance, justice, faith, hope, and love. We also highly disvalue (regret, repudiate, repent of, forgive) and refuse to identify ourselves with many other enduring states of our characters, that is, with such vices as imprudence, cowardice, overindulgence, unfairness, faithlessness, despair, hatred, and malice. None of these can exist only for a fraction of a second. Their very conception, as well as their realization and evaluation, require personal endurance and positive personal identification with enduring selfhood and its enduring properties. The intense concentration involved in significant creativity—like freeing the statue of David from the block of marble in which it is trapped—requires unified personal endurance and persistence. (By the way, the statue of David has no soul.) When we value non-trivial creativity, we are mainly valuing its endurance in ourselves and others over prolonged spans of time. The things that we value most profoundly in life endure significantly by degrees.

Inferring that wholes have a certain property (e.g., intrinsic worth) just because each part has that property commits the informal logical fallacy of composition, so we cannot infer logically that we as mere societies still in process have intrinsic worth just because all of our momentary parts or occasions do. By basically the same logic in reverse, the fallacy of division, we as enduring persons or soul-fields could have intrinsic worth even if none of our single occasions do. Standard process metaphysics gives an unsatisfactory analysis of the constitution and self-identity of inclusive human persons, or what Whitehead called "enduring individualities" (*AI* 279-82). *Strictly speaking, on his view, inclusive enduring persons are not individuals; we are societies.* We are vastly complex temporally enduring and spatially extended collections of momentary occasions unified by common and intimate strands of causation and psychological traits called "subjective forms." In more familiar language, our "souls" or "selves" have relative personal identity through time because our past feelings, purposes, desires, emotions, convictions, experiences, memories, etc., are repeated and included in our tenth-of-a-second-nows, and in what such fleeting occasions will be in the future. Nothing about us resides in our enduring souls *apart from* the successive occasions of our consciousness (or the consciousness of our brain cells). With that, I disagree.

I do agree with Brian Henning that one central challenge of process ethics is to develop a conception of macroscopic individuality that "is robust enough to do justice to the undeniable unity that we experience of ourselves and of other macroscopic individuals . . . when the actual occasions of which they are made do not endure" (67). A viable process ethics requires *enduring* self-and-other valuing soul-fields in process, as provided for in Chapter One of this book. If our past selves are active in our present selves, this is because they are essentially the same, except for ongoing temporal additions to or total property inventories. Whitehead thought that we are innumerably many momentary subjects, each having one experience. The soul-fields view shows how we can be one enduring subject having innumerably many experiences. Only such a view is robust enough to do justice to the undeniable unity that we experience of ourselves.

INDIVIDUALITY

Commenting on the era of the Christian Middle Ages, Whitehead noted that "The moral discipline had emphasized the intrinsic value of the individual entity. This emphasis had put the notions of the individual and of its experiences into the foreground of thought" (*SMW* 194). For Whitehead himself, "intrinsically good" applies most obviously and directly to *conscious individuals* who positively value something, perhaps themselves, but who are not blind to or unconcerned about the value of others and the whole. This brings us back to the metaphysical issue earlier discussed. If individuals have intrinsic worth, *what is an individual,* and which individuals really count for moral purposes?

For Whitehead, *"individual"* has *two radically different meanings. First,* the concept applies primarily to each numerically distinct, transient, *almost instantly perishing* actual occasion. *Next,* it applies secondarily to every numerically distinct *enduring* society of actual occasions, both to those that are personally ordered like human and animal souls, and to all persisting inanimate "things" or mere aggregates (*MT* 128). Whitehead wrote of "the importance of the individual" (*AI* 292), but what kind of individual did he have in mind, especially when affirming intrinsic importance? This may be hard to determine, but his emphasis on occasions, not enduring individuals, is clear enough in, "the occasion as an experience for its own sake" (*SMW* 170), "Morality is always the aim at that union of harmony, intensity, and vividness which involves the perfection of importance for that occasion" (*MT* 14), and "Morality emphasizes the detailed occasion" (*MT* 39). John Cobb clearly located intrinsic worth in occasions, not enduring individuals. "Intrinsic value," he wrote, "is the value of individual occasions of experience," and "Furthermore it must be in the subjective immediacy of the individual occasion that intrinsic value is to be found" (1965, 100).

With Brian Henning (156), I agree that *we are never morally concerned with individual actual occasions as such.* Even if they do have fleeting tenth-of-a-second intrinsic value, this is so trivial as to be of no ethical significance. Ephemeral actual occasions may have significance for themselves, but they have no moral and little if any other significance for us as real people. The scope of our moral concerns extend only to *enduring* and valuing conscious individuals like people and animals, to individuals with souls, to those having dominant enduring conscious psychophysical actualities within their bodies. Whitehead admitted that "Importance depends on endurance" (*SMW* 194), and he recognized "a sense of a unity of many occasions with a value beyond that of any individual occasion; for example, the soul" (*AI* 294). The trouble is, for Whitehead, value does not exceed the sum of *many* individual occasions. Also, many inanimate aggregate individuals endure, as he also acknowledged, so endurance alone is not sufficient for intrinsic worth. "Self-enjoyment," as Whitehead often expressed it (being an enjoying or valuing self or subject), is also required (*AI* 219). So is consciousness.

Henning makes considerable progress in showing that a Whiteheadian metaphysics must and can "do justice to the undeniable unity that we experience of ourselves and of other macroscopic individuals" (67 and most of his Ch. 3). Chapter One of the book you are now reading developed a field-based understanding of enduring human souls as subjects and agents that goes beyond Henning (and beyond Bracken) in order to strengthen Henning's commendable aim to do justice to ourselves on a macroscopic level. If, as he says, all "moral agents are macroscopic individuals" (74), this implies that no actual occasions are moral agents, and that macroscopic individuals have properties and powers that the sum of their occasions do not have. It implies that our human moral agency is something more than the sum of the moral agencies of the occasions within our personal stream of consciousness—since they don't have any moral agency at all. This is clearly a property that the whole has, but not any of our parts.

To do full justice to ourselves as intrinsically valuable moral agents, we need a better account of personal self-identity and agency through time. Without acknowledging or explicitly accepting his interpretation of human souls as fields, Henning agrees with Bracken about the "collective agency" of enduring human souls or "macroscopic individuals" (95-96, 213 n. 23), but it is not clear to me that either of them do full justice to "the undeniable unity that we experience of ourselves." Further development of the concept of the enduring soul as a unified, self-identical, self-valuing, enduring, fundamentally real agent-field is also required. This was supplied in the previous chapter.

UNIQUENESS

The concept of *"uniqueness"* adds something that "individuality" does not quite cover. Our uniqueness contributes significantly to our being final ends, valuable in, to, and for ourselves. It is not at all clear that "individuality" meant anything more for Whitehead than "numerical distinctness within a given class," but this alone does not capture the richness or complexity of the qualities and relations that are internal to each numerically distinct individual person or animal. Daniel A. Dombrowski was getting at the difference between numerical individuality and uniqueness when he wrote of animals,

> Relying on John Cobb, Hartshorne touches on another snag in our relations with animals. We value each human being individually, but "we tend to think that one nightingale or one hermit thrush is significant chiefly as a specimen of its species" [*Reality as Social Process,* 56]. . . . Although the death of a bird is very different from the death of a human being, we must keep in mind that Birdhood or Cowness never suffer, but *this* bird or *that* cow do. (1988, 78; see also 82-83, and Dombrowski 2001, 26.)

What Dombrowski says about animals is also true of human beings. "Humanity" or "human nature" never suffers or enjoys. Nor do numerically distinct individuals with only those defining properties ever suffer. Only this or that unique person does. Instances of "humanity" may be replaced without loss of those defining properties, e.g., "rational animal," or their worth. Unique individuals, each one of a kind, cannot. There is considerable ambiguity about uniqueness and replaceability in current process ethics, but there should not be. Yes, each numerically distinct specimen of a kind or species is an individual, but we are missing something ethically significant when we take only that into account and do not further consider the full definiteness of their uniqueness. For Whitehead, enduring individuals are numerically distinct instances of the class of societies of actual occasions that inherit data and subjective forms primarily from a single line of antecedents, but it is not clear that he ever meant anything more than this. The trouble is, this tells us nothing of the nature or the value of our own personal uniqueness, or that of animals and other unique self-or-other valuing realities. Hartmanian axiology adds an in-depth analysis of uniqueness to Whitehead's numerically distinct individuality.

So what does this axiology say about uniqueness? For one thing, uniqueness is another important defining characteristic of all intrinsically valuable entities. This claim clearly goes beyond Whitehead. According to Robert S. Hartman, *"uniqueness"* means both *"having all the properties we have"* and *"having properties that nothing else has"* (Edwards 2010, 56-61). Hartman recognized that every person is unique and that our intrinsic goodness is tied to our uniqueness. (We must add that this is true also of animals.) Formal Axiology, he said, affirms that the "highest value is the individual" (1967, 254), but here he clearly meant "unique individual." Hartman held that "Unique" is the value category that belongs distinctively to the realm of intrinsic value, the highest form of value; extrinsic "goodness" of a kind belongs to instrumental or useful values; "perfection" belongs to all-or-nothing systemic or conceptual values (199).

Hartman himself struggled to achieve a satisfactory understanding of uniqueness. According to Hartman, uniqueness is not a property of an entity; it is a property of its properties, specifically, the *completeness* of its total set of properties. "Unique," he first wrote, means that an entity has "all the properties that it has" (1960, 15), but even that is not enough. If we go no further, this definition is inadequate, especially if "uniqueness" is supposed to distinguish intrinsically good things from those that are merely extrinsically or systemically good. All concretely existing things have all the properties that they have, whether individual persons, individual rocks, or individual concepts. "Uniqueness" *also* usually means "having properties, or configurations of properties, that nothing else has," as Hartman also acknowledged eventually (1967, 60). Even in this sense, human selves are not uniquely unique. All existing bricks and thoughts are thus unique, if only with respect to having their distinctive loci in spacetime, or their distinctive meanings, that nothing else has. Whitehead recognized that each "eternal object" (each systemic concept or its referent, Hartman might say) is thus unique. According to Whitehead, eternal objects (universals, we might say) have "uniqueness," for "Each eternal object is an individual which, in its own peculiar fashion, is what it is" (*SMW* 159) and "Any eternal object is just itself" (171). Both "all" and "distinctive" properties are required for uniqueness.

Consider further our distinctiveness. Not having some important things in common with others is one of the most important things that we all have in common! No human being is only generically human, having only the defining property of "rational animal," or "featherless biped" (or whatever works to define us). No human being has *only* abstract generic capacities for consciousness, self-consciousness, valuation, intelligence, feelings and affections, creative choice-making, etc. Concretely, all of us have properties that no one else has. Although our total property inventories exemplify ingressed eternal objects that are also present in other unique individuals, our total sets of properties are configured in each of us in an absolutely distinctive manner. Value combinations matter greatly. All of us are unique individuals, one of a kind, unrepeated and unrepeatable under the sun, and our uniqueness is one of our most important intrinsic-good-making properties. Of course, uniqueness alone does not fully account for our intrinsic worth because, in a sense, all mindless thoughts and things are also unique, that is, all are just what they are and have at least one property that nothing else has; and they may be so regarded and valued. As Whitehead understood, "Every so called 'universal' is particular in the sense of being just what it is, diverse from everything else" (*PR* 48).

No single instance of our five defining properties of "intrinsically good" is sufficient unto itself. Uniqueness is *one* essential good-making property of all intrinsically good entities, but it cannot be their only intrinsic-good-making property. All intrinsically good entities (e.g., persons) are unique, but not all unique entities (e.g., ideas, or bricks, or other material things) are intrinsically good. Only unique actualities that *also* exemplify other properties like endurance, consciousness, valuation or self or others, thinking, deciding, feeling, creativity/freedom, etc., have intrinsic worth. Intrinsically good actualities are a synthesis of uniqueness with additional intrinsic-good-making properties like valuation of self or others, consciousness, endurance, and numerical individuality. Just how far these properties extend into the depths of the non-human world is an ongoing topic of lively debate, especially among process thinkers. So what are some of our uniquely individuating or unshared properties?

1. All actualized universals or ingressed eternal objects within us are concretely combined or configured in each person in an absolutely unique way (as are our fingerprints, iris eye patterns, genes, etc).

2. Each person has his or her own distinctive total property inventory.

3. Every person occupies an absolutely unique and unrepeatable position in space and time. No one else was ever born exactly where and when I was born, and no one else sits exactly where I sit as I now type these words. This spatiotemporal uniqueness extends throughout our lives. Human spatiotemporality involves unique embodiment; no one else has my body; no one else has yours.

4. Every person constantly enjoys an absolutely unique and distinctive perspective on the universe. No one else ever sees or otherwise experiences anything from exactly my point of view, so my every experience is unique. Whitehead recognized the significance of "the perspective of the universe for that entity" (*MT* 66).

5. All persons make their own choices. No one else makes them for us, or makes them at all. Each new choice is an additional value-making property, as is every other new positive experience. Every good decision we make adds to our total inventory of positive or good-for-us properties. Time constantly enriches our axiological goodness, our total inventory of good-making properties.

6 What was just said of choice is also true of all previously discussed universally human intrinsic-good-making properties in the concrete. Each person is consciously and self-consciously unique with respect to all the *details* of self-enjoyment, consciousness and self-consciousness, and all the particulars of functioning intelligence, affections, and actions. In the abstract, we have many desirable general capacities in common; in particular, mine are only mine, and yours are only yours.

7. Considered concretely rather than in the abstract, all of us have our own distinctive personal projects, stations in life, and responsibilities to ourselves and others. Here and now, no one else has exactly my

possibilities, my moral duties, or my responsibilities for the future, and I and I alone must decide and do.

8. Each of us has a distinctive set of friends, family, and intimates to love and care for, and no one else loves and cares for them in exactly the way each of us does.

9. Each of us has a unique knowledge/ignorance inventory, and a unique set of practical abilities/inabililties.

10. All of us have our own unique self-concepts, self-knowledge, self-ideals, and self-expectations, and we fulfill them or fail to do so in our own distinctive ways. We can measure our own axiological worth by the degree to which we fulfill our unique self-expectations and are thus authentic and true to ourselves.

11. Each of us can only die once in, to, and for ourselves. Nobody else can do it for me. No one else can do it for you.

Consider now how having *all* of our properties is essential to our uniqueness. The best Hartmanian concept of "*unique individual* human personhood" I have been able to formulate is: "A unique individual person is the integrated totality of all of his or her properties (qualities and relations)" (Edwards 2010, 58). In short, we are "our total property inventory," and *this includes* our soul-field and all the properties (eternal objects) that we do and do not have in common with all other persons. It includes the defining properties of "humanity," but much more. Hartman himself came very close to expressing this definition when he wrote of "x's self, i.e. the integral totality of all of x's attributes" (1991, 15). Process thinkers would also agree that all the temporal occasions of our past, present, and future belong to the total property inventories of our enduring personally ordered soul-societies. Much that Hartman wrote adds up to this, but to much more. He clearly regarded enduring individual persons in their full determinateness, concreteness, and uniqueness as intrinsically good, in contrast with the extrinsic goodness of inanimate things in our public sensory world, and the systemic worth of mere ideas, concepts, and beliefs.

Predicates (mental concepts) and their corresponding properties (in objects), as understood by Hartman, obviously relate closely to "eternal objects," as understood by Whitehead (*SMW* Ch. X). Eternal objects initially are only relational possibilities for actualization, located first in the Primordial Nature or Mind of God. They may also come to exist concretely within actualities in our real world, and then be absorbed ultimately into God's Consequent Nature. Real embodied people consist of their temporally ordered sets of concrete, determinate, ingressed, predicate/properties or eternal objects, as well as their distinctive soul-fields.

Throughout this discussion, I assume that Charles Hartshorne was correct in holding that actual existence adds a definiteness, determinateness, concreteness, "thisness," or something to eternal objects that they do not have in themselves as mere possibilities (1972, 31-34, 59, 95-97). This is why real people have much more value than their mere possibilities, even if both contain identical sets of eternal objects (predicates or their corresponding properties). Mere possibilities lack the concreteness or complete definiteness that is integral to our actuality and uniqueness. This is perhaps the real significance of the enigmatic philosophical judgment, "Existence is not a predicate." Existence or actuality is not just another eternal object or set of such alongside all the others. Nevertheless, it really makes a difference! When we don't have it, we are either unborn or dead!

Perhaps enough has been said to make the essential point about uniqueness, though we will return to our "total property inventory" in a later section on "Who or What Am I?" We are not intrinsically good simply because we are generically human and share "humanity," whatever that is. In addition, we are numerically distinct persons or human beings, but more than this is required. We are valuable in, to, for, and because of our absolute uniqueness. Ethically, we can and should value all persons as one of a kind and not just as generically human or numerically distinct. Values that are not unique, e.g., our defining common human properties, and our social roles, are replaceable without loss of goodness by any other individual who exemplifies those properties to the same degree. Real people are not.

REPLACEABILITY

Replaceability is the key ethical consideration that separates individuality from uniqueness. Mere individuals, numerically distinct specimens of a species or class, may be replaced without loss of worth; unique individuals cannot. Unique individuals are *one of a kind,* thus not replaceable. Numerically distinct individuals are one of a class and are replaceable (Edwards 1991, 97-101; Dombrowski, 2001, 22-35). In *Matters of Life and Death,* John Cobb considers, but ultimately rejects, the following reply to the argument that destroying whole species of non-human life is wrong because "intrinsic value is being destroyed."

> But this is not necessarily the case. With the extinction of one species, others may multiply. There may be no reduction in the total quantity of intrinsic value in the world. Indeed, if the extinction of other species makes possible a larger human population, then it could be replied that the total amount of intrinsic value is increased (41).

This same line of argument could be applied to the wrongness of killing *individual* persons (and animals) as well as to *species.* To paraphrase with respect to persons: With the extinction of one individual person, others may multiply. There may be no reduction of intrinsic value in the world. Indeed, if the extinction of one individual person makes possible a larger human population, then it could be replied that the total amount of intrinsic value is increased. In other words, no intrinsic value would be lost where one numerically distinct person is replaced by at least one other individual person, or better yet even more than one. But is this really true? Do any of us who know him really believe that John Cobb could ever be replaced?! He will have successors, but never a replacement! When Thomas Jefferson followed Benjamin Franklin as our Ambassador to France, he was asked if he was Franklin's replacement. He replied, "No one can replace him, sir; I am only his successor" (Mayo 1942, 115). That goes right to the point!

So, intrinsic value would be lost if one intrinsically valuable person is killed and replaced by another. If intrinsic goodness would be diminished by such killing, sheer numerical individuality does not account for this. Uniqueness does.

It is logically possible that many distinct individuals in some class are almost exactly alike except for being numerically different. Atoms and electrons, for example, come very close to fitting this description. There is little or no novelty or creativity in them. They repeat their self-valued patterns or subjective forms almost endlessly, with very little "swerving," as Epicurus put it. Quantum physics allows for a tiny bit of such unpredictability, indefiniteness, and discontinuity, where Newtonian physics did not (*SMW* 34-36, 135-36). Uniqueness involves far more than numerical difference, however. What unique individuals have in common is that they are all somehow different! Even then, their full richness of positive properties varies immensely within and between unique individuals. There is very little of it in atoms and electrons, much more of it as we go up the scale of intrinsically valuable actualities, but even we wax and wane in good-making properties.

If individual persons have only *extrinsic or systemic worth,* they can be replaced without loss of value or goodness. However, unique persons cannot be replaced without loss of *intrinsic* worth. Very often we relate to unique persons and animals as if they have only systemic or extrinsic worth, that is, very often we evaluate them only extrinsically or systemically. Except for our beloved pets, we evaluate almost all animals extrinsically (e.g., as bacon or beef) or systemically (e.g., as sources of numbered dollars). For extrinsic and systemic purposes, one animal is just as good or profitable as another with the same properties. Unless we have formed intimate personal relations with them, most people in our lives are also replaceable with little or no sense of loss. This is because in practice we usually evaluate people only extrinsically or systemically. All extrinsic and systemic value-objects are replaceable without loss by something or someone else just as good. We can and often do attach value to other persons and animals (intrinsic values) *only* for their usefulness (as extrinsic values) or for ideological or monetary reasons (as systemic values). Ethically, this leaves a lot to be desired.

We do not normally grieve when our students, colleagues, customers, employers, employees, etc. move on or away and are no longer in our lives. We can always get another one if their value to us is merely extrinsic or systemic. They are replaceable individuals. We do grieve, however, when those who are very close to us, those we value intimately, intrinsically and uniquely, move away or out of our lives, especially when separated by death. If we did not cherish uniqueness, we would feel no great loss when a dear friend or loved one dies, just as a shopkeeper feels no great loss when a customer walks away. Yet, this is not so; we do grieve when intimates are lost.

But can't dear friends and loved ones also be replaced without loss by other friends and loved ones, just like passing customers or most of the students in last year's classes? Not so. Grief focuses primarily on unique individuals, not just on numerical individuality, common humanity, repeatable social roles, usefulness to self or others, or systemic ideological class and conformity. Friends and loved ones may have beneficial *successors,* but they cannot be *replaced* intrinsically. There is a reduction of intrinsic value of the world with the extinction of one irreplaceable unique person (or animal), even if other individuals partly fill the void. If we comprehend that, we have understood the value of unique and intrinsically valuable persons and animals and how uniqueness is essential to all intrinsic worth.

WHO OR WHAT AM I?

A philosophical consideration about "Who or what am I?" may help to show how "having all of my properties" and "having properties that no one else has" (the meanings of "uniqueness") are essential to having intrinsic worth. This question can be asked and answered by everyone, so the "I" used here is everyone's "I." According to formal axiology's understanding of "self," *I am the integrated unity and totality of all of my properties,* including those no one else has, and whether these are good or bad (Edwards, 2010, 58-61). Hartman thought that our proper names have meaning, specifically our total property inventory. To know who we are, the meaning of our proper names, we have to know everything that there is to know about ourselves, and only God knows that.

Part of the problem is that none of us are finished or completed integrated totalities. Our metaphysical "satisfactions" are definite but not complete. We exist in time. We are becomings, not mere beings. Every moment adds new and interesting good-making (or bad-making) properties to our integrated totality of properties. Time perpetually perishes, but it also perpetually creates new sensory and introspected experiences, new thoughts and beliefs, sensations, feelings, desires, appetites, emotions, purposes, interests, moods, attitudes, approvals, enjoyments, loyalties, etc., as well as new choices and new creative intellectual, moral, artistic, and practical endeavors. Time constantly adds to the richness of who "I" am, to the richness and distinctiveness of my total concrete intrinsic-good-making properties, to the richness of the meaning of my proper name. So it is with all of us.

The *number* of good-making properties in the abstract *definition* of "humanity," (e.g., "rational animal," "featherless biped," or whatever), can be counted easily; but the *number* of the good-making properties in unique individuals is so vast that counting them is practically impossible. In addition, we have bad-making properties that must also be counted, for they also belong to the meanings of our proper names. Hartman himself insisted that intrinsically valuable people have more than just a practically uncountable number of good-making properties. We have an actual infinity of them because we can think an infinite number of thoughts, he claimed. I vehemently opposed his "argument for the infinite value of man" from the moment I first heard it, and I have published my objections to it in several places (e.g., Edwards, 1973, 141-47; 2010, 70-85). We just can't actually think an infinite number of thoughts. I finally realized after many years, however, that the really good stuff in Hartmanian axiology can be separated from its occasional absurdities.

Unique human beings, Hartman acknowledged, are constantly and freely creative, thus constantly both temporal and enduring. Some people are much more creative than others. "The vast majority of men stop at narrow ranges of creativity," he wrote (278). In time, we make free choices that are conditioned but not determined by antecedents. Thereby, we are moral agents and are morally responsible for what we are, choose, think, feel, and do. The temporality of the human self is more implicit in some of Hartman's writings than others, though usually this is explicit enough. His whole axiological psychology was about human self-development and self-creation through time in multiple value dimensions. It pinpoints human shortcomings when self-development in three value dimensions takes place asymmetrically, or does not take place as it should. He regularly emphasized the relationality of selfhood, often quoting with admiration Kierkegaard's definition of the self as "a relation which relates itself to its own self" (1962, 418). Hartman was not always as crystal clear about the temporality of human selfhood as he should have been, as I explained elsewhere (Edwards 1995, 41-50), so this is one place where process thought can contribute valid insight and clarity to Hartmanian philosophy.

Process thinkers maintain that we are "relational" selves, as reflected in the titles, subject matter, and contents of many recent books and articles. We are largely constituted by subjective forms, purposes, aims, and data inherited through causal relations with a vast plethora of events in our past, especially our most immediate past. These include our own past free and creative decisions, God's loving nurturing and nudging us toward what is best, our genetic and bodily endowment, our social relations with other people and living creatures, our supportive biosphere and physical environment, and the influence of a vast portion of the antecedent universe. The universe has prepared for our coming for at least 14.7 billion years. The focus is on time. If Hartmanian "selfhood" is to be reconciled with process selfhood, being "the integrated totality of all of our properties, both qualitative and relational," must be qualified emphatically by temporality or becoming.

"Having all of our properties" is not a done deal. At any given moment, we have a vast plethora of properties, both actual and possible, but our total set of actual properties is unfinished until death do us depart. Aristotle suggested that no one could be *completely* happy until he (or she) is dead, because something bad might happen in the future to spoil everything. Without getting bogged down in that, we should readily agree that none of us have all of our self-fulfilling properties *completely* until we are dead, and not even then if there is survival after death involving new events or happenings. We are temporally ordered selves, and "our total property inventory" is unfinished as long as we live, maybe even forever if there is "subjective immortality" or survival after death re-embodied in some spacetime system somewhere. Process is integral to our reality.

Hartman wrote, "The outstanding feature of a dead person is that nothing happens with him anymore, that he is no source any more of properties or features" (1968, 43). He and process thinkers agree that we are appreciably free and self-creative. With God, we are responsible co-creators of ourselves; what our future selves will be like depends significantly on the decisions that we make here and now in the subjective immediacy, freedom, creativity, and independence of our present moments of what Whitehead called "sheer individuality" (*AI* 177). He thought that it is "in this immediate present, that an occasion finds its own originality" (*SMW* 176).

Formal axiology contributes significantly to answering, "Who or what am I?" Hartman thought that we are the same persons through time, partly because our souls endure, but largely because our values and our patterns of valuation tend to persist. Persisting values and evaluations alone are not enough. As argued earlier, we are enduring, empowered, and creative soul-fields, and our souls have ontological as well as psychological continuity or sameness through time. We are both the same and changing—constantly. What and how we value, our values and valuations, help to make us who and what we are now and over time. We have relative stable personalities, but we also change physically and psychologically, and we increase in total richness of positive (or negative) properties while remaining fundamentally the same persons ontologically.

As more carefully explained later, Hartmanian formal axiology recognizes three distinct kinds or dimensions of goodness. Our personal-value-making properties belong to three basic kinds of goodness—systemic, extrinsic, and intrinsic. Our human personalities are organized around all three, not just one, and our values are the real keys to our personalities. We are partly feelings but also partly thoughts, choices, and actions. We inherit and transmit to the future not only common intrinsic subjective forms of feeling (purposes, feelings, emotions, desires), but also extrinsic physical properties (embodied processes and behavioral propensities), and persisting systemic properties (ideas, thoughts, convictions, patterns, and beliefs). We now know how to rank all of these values, and all are integral parts of our total property inventories, our unique personal worth and overall well-being.

Systemic properties are thought properties—ideas, concepts, words, beliefs, rules, principles, laws, ritual forms, mathematics, logic, and the likes of such. Philosophical, theological, and scientific belief systems are composed of systemic properties. To the extent that they are within us, they partly constitute who we are, our total property inventory, our uniqueness, and our well-being. We are partly composed of systemic value objects. As we think and learn conceptually, our personal inventory of systemic good-making properties is enriched. Education increases the systemic aspects of our unique personalities.

Extrinsic properties are spatiotemporal properties that exist in our common perceptual world of spacetime. Philosophers traditionally defined "extrinsic values" in terms of actual or potential usefulness. Hartman understood extrinsic values to be actually or potentially useful things, processes, and activities located in our common, public, perceptual spacetime world. Aggregates, colors, odors, sounds, tastes, shapes, sizes, motions, human bodies, etc., and all their actual and possible uses and combinations, no matter how intricate, are extrinsic or external properties. Extrinsic values, or their physical conditions, first exist outside of human consciousness, then enter into human consciousness when experienced. We value things in public spacetime as extrinsic values to the degree that they satisfy our practical expectations of them, that is, to the degree that they fulfill the standards of usefulness we apply to them. Our bodies, as experienced through sensory perception, consist of extrinsic sensory properties that are integral parts of our total personal property inventories, thus integral aspects of who we really are. Our bodies are useful to us. As we nurture, use, and care for our bodies, we are further enriched with good-making extrinsic properties. We are not mere souls; we are also our bodies. To be true to ourselves and fulfill ourselves as embodied souls, we become athletes, gardeners, builders, hikers, players, drinkers, diners, or physically active in some way. All of our physical activities enrich our total property inventories and well-being. Physical activity, fitness, and health are good for us. We have an immediate sense of the "withness" of our bodies, as well as a sensory awareness of them.

We live in a spatiotemporal universe, a physical environment of sensory things and processes that can enrich (or impoverish) our experiences and our lives. As we take the properties of objectively existing spatiotemporal things into ourselves in sensory perception, affective appreciation, and aesthetic enjoyment, they become integral aspects of who we are. They become parts of ourselves, our extrinsic selves. To the extent that mere things fulfill our expectations and the standards we apply to them, they are extrinsically good, and they enrich our lives. Matter is good, not bad, though anything can be overvalued, undervalued, or disvalued.

Intrinsic properties in *one sense* include *all* of our properties, for all dimensions of value are taken up into our intrinsic, complete, personal uniqueness. Our uniqueness includes *all* our systemic, extrinsic, and distinctively intrinsic properties, our total property inventories, as well as our ontologically enduring soul-fields. Our distinctively internal properties are integral parts of who we are intrinsically, but so are our systemic and extrinsic properties, for we are complete human beings, not immaterial souls. Our total enduring actuality, including all our properties, qualities, relations, and their configurations make us *unique* ends to, in, and for ourselves.

In *another sense* some of our properties are *distinctively intrinsic*. That is, they do not belong to our systemic and external extrinsic property inventories—for example, consciousness, immediate self-awareness, and all of our psychological properties, capacities, and activities. These include our freedom, creativity, love, empathy, compassion, valuation, and identification with ourselves, others, the universe, and God. Distinctively intrinsic properties include all of our internal intrinsic, extrinsic, and systemic evaluations. They include our distinctive internal properties, our spiritual and moral virtues—sensing the presence of God, fulfilling our self-expectations, being true to ourselves, exercising self-control, being courageous, fair, just, moderate, considerate, faithful, devoted, loving, compassionate, hopeful, honest, sincere, trustworthy, and the like. All of these enter into answering, "Who am I?"

As we intensify and develop our internal distinctively intrinsic properties, capacities, activities, and experiences, we are enriched with the most desirable and fulfilling good-making properties of all. Our distinctively intrinsic psychological and evaluational properties are the cores of our personalities. Through time they change, develop, increase, and enrich our total goodness and well-being. As enduring and changing souls, we grow spiritually, morally, affectively, intellectually, and practically as time marches on.

We are embodied, spatiotemporally extended, and enduring souls, each with our own distinctive causal inheritance and physical and psychological structures, relations, qualities, values, concreteness, and inclusive uniqueness. We are not non-spatial immaterial soul substances temporarily imprisoned in our bodies. Whitehead identified the human "soul" with our human stream of consciousness, that is, with what he called the "dominant personal society" within our bodies. "The soul is nothing else than the succession of my occasions of experience, extending from birth to present moment. Now, at this instant, *I am the complete person embodying all these occasions*" (*MT* 163, italics added). Souls are inherently embodied and inclusive, and Whitehead's own words recognize this. Our intimate sense or feeling of union with our bodies is a "primary experience," he declared. Soul/body unity is a basic reality. Both bodies and souls are integral parts of who we are. We normally take this for granted without lapsing into Platonic/Cartesian mind-matter dualism. In axiological terms, our extrinsic selves (I vegetate and act, etc., therefore, I am) are just as much a part of our total property inventories as our inner affective/appetitive selves (I feel, desire, love, etc., therefore, I am) and our systemic rational selves (I think, therefore, I am). If being a unique, enduring, actual/potential field of consciousness is one of our properties, that, too, is included.

Whitehead conceived of "personal unity" or "personal identity" along lines remarkably similar to axiology's "total property inventory. He compared it not to Plato's immaterial "Soul," but to Plato's "Receptacle," the repository of all natural events. He wrote, "Personal identity is the thing which receives all occasions of the man's existence" (*AI* 187). Yes, he regarded each individual occasion as having intrinsic importance, but what about our total property inventory? What about the inclusive "I," our total unique enduring personal unity or identity? Whitehead's answer is fuzzy, if it can be found at all, and so it is with most process thinkers. This book argues that we as inclusive enduring embodied souls have intrinsic worth.

In the end, we decide that our total property inventory (our unique enduring soul-field plus all our qualities and relations) has intrinsic worth in the same way we decide that our fleeting moments have intrinsic worth. Namely, we find after careful, calm, and persistent consideration that this axiomatic judgment accords with our deepest, most enduring, and most carefully considered value intuitions. Carefully considered and refined judgments and determinations of intrinsic worth are so basic that they cannot be derived logically from anything else even more basic. Still, we can say and think things that help bring these intuitions up into the light of consciousness for careful consideration. In Chapter Four, G.E. Moore's "Method of Isolation" for identifying intrinsically valuable entities will be explored, but all of our basic value axioms depend in the end on our carefully considered axiological intuitions. God, working through evolution and human nature, provides us with very basic axiological and moral intuitions (conscience) as a way of luring us toward what is best.

Valuing our unique, enduring, unified, conscious individualities intrinsically means partly that we fulfill our self-ideals, and partly that we intensely identify ontologically, psychologically, and affectively with our own total past, present, and future realities. Abnormality excepted, we strongly identify with our enduring selves. The standard process view of the self as nothing more than a society of momentary occasions harbors unresolved puzzles about the unity, fundamental reality, agency, and value of unique enduring souls. As noted previously, there is a puzzle about how present actual occasions can be and feel responsible for past decisions and actions when these were made by different actual occasions long since perished. How can a present-self-occasion be concerned about distinct future-self-occasions that do not yet exist? The answer must be that after careful consideration we identify axiologically and psychologically with our ontologically unified and enduring past, present and future selves. Something very real about us and in the ultimate nature of things warrants this.

According to Hartman, intrinsic evaluation of ourselves involves fulfilling our concepts of our continuing selves, realizing our "self-concepts," "self-images," "self-ideals," or "plans of life" as they are often called, over the course of time. This happens only over the long run, never in single actual occasions, for our self-concepts grow and change. Unified, aware, enduring, unique individuality is what really matters to us, and process thought needs to account better for this. We care deeply about our real potentialities over the long run, not just about our present actualities. Sadly, many people are very shortsighted. Their long run is not very long, but moral and spiritual growth consists largely in expanding the extent of this long run. When we love ourselves and our neighbors, we identify intensely with unified, enduring, unique, embodied souls. Moral turpitude greatly inhibits love, and mental illness may distort it.

Developing and evaluating our enduring individuality and uniqueness are lengthy processes, and they often require the help of nurturing others. Personal growth and self-valuation take time and are not accomplished in or by a momentary self-occasion. Whitehead insisted that thinking "United Fruit Company" takes time, requires ongoing intentions and attentiveness, and is not accomplished in an instant (*AI* 182). The most important judgments that we make about ourselves, our cognitive self-valuations, take time—judgments like "I did a bad thing," "I am responsible for doing a bad thing," "I am true (or untrue) to myself," "I love myself," "I love you," "I love God," etc. No single actual occasion can think such thoughts, but I can. The cognitive aspects of evaluation are very significant to us, but they are not accomplished in a tenth of a second. Moral and spiritual growth, becoming a good person, fulfilling our best concepts of ourselves, finding ourselves, self-realization, all take time and involve ourselves as unique, enduring soul-fields.

THE VALUE OF AGGREGATES

Whitehead wrote, "Everything has some value for itself, for others, and for the whole" (*MT* 111). He had actual occasions, brief pulsations of becoming, in mind when he wrote this, so we should not take it too literally and without many qualifications. The entities, properties, and virtues to which we actually attach value are enduring personal and perceptual actualities and processes. Whitehead's "everything" applies most obviously only to unique, enduring, experiencing people and animals, not to non-living, or to non-experiencing aggregates like boulders and buildings. Their value is primarily instrumental, not intrinsic, as Brian Henning recognized (157). People and animals have or are souls. They are intense, complex, creative, consciously experiencing, valuing, dominant, enduring actual entities within their bodies. Aggregates are just bodies without souls.

Our Whiteheadian exuberance over non-sensory perception in the mode of causal efficacy (introspection) and the universality of self-significance should not blind us to the fact that the souls of most people are dominated most of the time by value-objects delivered to them through their "five external senses." Expressed more technically, most of us are dominated by, pay attention to, and commonly attach great significance to inanimate macroscopic sensory objects given to us in the mode of presentational immediacy. A dominant value orientation toward external useful sensory objects, processes, happenings, and actions has great evolutionary significance. It is good for survival and reproduction. It is very natural. It is in our genes. Early human beings who were too inward, introspective, and oriented toward Whiteheadian perception in the mode of causal efficacy, did not survive or reproduce, so no one is descended from them.

Most important for our purposes, *inanimate aggregates or macroscopic material objects*—houses, cars, boulders, buildings, cars, cash, sculptures, paintings, songs, gold watches, guns, diamond rings, mindless material objects of every description—*have no souls*. Even *sex-objects* are regarded and treated as if they have no souls. Macroscopic-level things, soul-less aggregates, *are indeed vacuous realities.* Regarding and treating them as vacuous actualities is not at all inappropriate, even if their ingredient electrons, atoms, and molecules have an exceedingly small degree of self-significance. Sensory experience filters out most of this. "Sense perception," said Whitehead, "omits any discrimination of the fundamental activities within nature" (*MT* 154). There is something illusory or at least superficial about sensory perception, and concentrating exclusively or primarily on it distracts us from our senses of temporality, the immediate past, bodily feelings, and of inner awareness and self-awareness (*MT* 133, 153-54). It also disregard the inwardness of others. It is oblivious to both small and large souls. Sensations only skim the surface of the so called "external world." They do not penetrate its depths. They filter out far more than they disclose.

Nevertheless, aggregates deserve an honored and respected place in process ethics, as long as they are not overvalued. Many sensory soul-less *macroscopic* material or physical resources are very desirable, very good, very beautiful and harmonious, but their macroscopic goodness is only instrumental, not intrinsic. Having extrinsic values is not unethical, as long as they are not ranked over intrinsic values. If individual atoms in cars and sculptures, and if cells in all bodies and microbes, have very small degrees of evaluational consciousness and intrinsic worth, this is considerably less than that of human and animal souls. For ethical purposes their intrinsic worth can and should be ignored. Why do they have less value? Because far fewer intrinsic-good-making properties are present in them in degree, kind, and duration. As Whitehead noted, "How incapable the separate cells and pulsations of each flower are of enjoying the total effect" (*MT* 120).

Except for degrees of endurance and numerical distinctness, mere things, macroscopic *non-living sense objects,* lack the good-making properties of intrinsically valuable unique individuals. Unique, enduring, conscious, valuing individuals have value for themselves and they value others; but enduring sensory physical aggregates have no awareness, consciousness, or values at all. They do not value themselves; they do not value others; they do not value anything. They mean nothing to themselves. Except for living bodies, enduring sense objects are mindless *aggregates,* as Whitehead clearly recognized (*SMW* 110), and as Hartshorne explained more carefully (1970, 33-34, 112, 142-43). Whitehead thought that most trees, plants, and vegetables are democracies of cells, do not have dominant souls, thus do not have any significance for themselves, even if their *living cells* do have minuscule self-significance. This claim may need further refinement.

Majestic mountains, oceans, and boulders, glorious sunsets, glamorous clothes, haunting songs, fabulous paintings and sculptures, and exquisite buildings like the Parthenon and the Cathedral of Notre Dame, are beautiful and harmonious; but they have no souls, no significance in, to, or for themselves, no "sakes" of their own. They mean nothing to themselves; they do not value themselves or anything else. They are soul-less aggregates, not self or other valuing individuals. They contain no dominant conscious societies or actual entities; they even lack living cells. They merely provide physically necessary, practically supportive, and aesthetically attractive sensory environments for living and valuing actualities. We should not allow our well placed concern for the environment to blind us to the fact that "the land," understood purely physically and macroscopically, has no intrinsic worth. Only the hoards of living things that depend on it do.

Some environmentalists attribute intrinsic worth to the land and regard it as sacred, but these are two different perspectives. The spiritual should not be confused initially with the ethical, even if they come together in the end. Only confusion results if we infer that macroscopic material objects and processes as wholes (e.g., landmasses as such) have intrinsic worth because their microscopic parts (e.g., their atoms, electrons, living inhabitants, etc.) have intrinsic worth. From a spiritual perspective, the land and all macroscopic material objects and processes are sacred because God created them and is present in them (omnipresence). Even so, they have no significance to themselves, thus no intrinsic worth, and we have no ethical duties to them as such. We are ethically obligated to protect and preserve beautiful aggregates because they mean so much to us, not because they mean anything to themselves. Nothing means anything to them at all. *Macroscopic-level* sensory grains of soil, land masses, boulders, buildings, sunrises, physical works of music and art, and other inanimate and unensouled inanimate "things" are indeed vacuous aggregates. They have no inwardness of their own, no intrinsic worth, no matter how beautiful, useful, or essential they are for us and other living things. Their goodness is instrumental, not intrinsic. They are only useful physical resources, but still very valuable as such.

What a "land ethic" actually values is not land itself (dirt) but the ecosystem or complex biosystem that occupies the land. As Dombrowski points out, "This conception deprives individuals of any value except as they contribute to the biotic community . . . and it grants no additional value to rationality or even to sentiency except as they might contribute to the community" (47). Land ethics turns unique, conscious, self-valuing individuals into mere means to the ends of a greater biosphere that is not a conscious individual and has no ends.

Macroscopic land is a very significant extrinsic good, but only the living individuals it supports are intrinsically good. The point that macrocosmic-level material or sensory objects have only instrumental worth is not at all trivial or morally and spiritually irrelevant. For one thing, recognizing this significantly qualifies the "everything" in Whitehead's, "*Everything* has some value for itself, for others, and for the whole." "Everything," taken literally, does not have significance for itself.

WORLDLY OVERVALUATION OF AGGREGATES

Many people attach excessive value to, and mistakenly attribute intrinsic worth to, merely mindless things, to soul-less aggregates. Jonathan Edwards, John Wesley, Søren Kierkegaard and many theologians through the ages properly stress this. They called such axiologically warped people "worldly" (Edwards 2012a, Ch. 3; and 2012b, Ch. 1). Worldly people do not find God in the things of the world. Their primary values are mindless or soul-less macroscopic material objects or aggregates. They value them intrinsically for their own sakes. They greatly overvalue the things of the world, and they are insensitive to the value of inwardness, which they lack. They love inanimate things far more than they love God, people, animals, and living things. Weakness in non-sensuous inner perception is a serious moral, spiritual, and epistemological defect. Many very ordinary people value mere things, soul-less material objects, as if they have intrinsic worth, as if they have souls. They value the non-valuing things of the world with all their own hearts, and souls, and minds, and strength. As theologians appropriately indicate, this is sheer idolatry.

"Materialism" is also moral perversity. Valuing mere things as if they were people, and people as if they were mere things, and acting accordingly, is both ethical and spiritual corruption. Many people live primarily for soul-less things like houses, cars, clothes, trinkets, tools, computers, smart phones, music, and innumerable other macroscopic physical resources. They love material things that cannot love them back much more than they love God, people, and animals who could love them back. The values that form their souls are very distorted, so their souls are very distorted. They do not hesitate to exploit, injure, and destroy people, animals, and their supporting environments to gain the world, that is, to obtain more and more mindless things for themselves. These unethical people overvalue mere things and undervalue people, animals, and other living things. They rank extrinsic values over intrinsic values.

Inner non-sensuous perception in the mode of causal efficacy is very real, but many people have little awareness of it because they are extrinsically and psychologically oriented toward sensory perception in the mode of presentational immediacy. Some philosophers ground epistemology and their theories of reality and value (or valuelessness) solely on sensory experiences. Hume and the Positivists did that, according to Whitehead, and so does much of modern natural science.

Whitehead had some grasp of the degree to which the souls of many ordinary people are dominated and corrupted by sensory values. He discerned how much we tend to love the soul-less things of the world, mere aggregates, overvalue mindless macroscopic objects, and undervalue intrinsic value objects like individual human beings. He was convinced that in addition to "the natural greed of mankind," both "scientific materialism" and a political economy fixed on "commercial affairs" contribute significantly to today's commonplace overvaluation of sensory objects and processes. The psychological gap between "only material things are real" and "only material things have value" is very thin. Whitehead did not use the word "worldliness" for it, but here is how he addressed modern manifestations of it.

> In regard to the aesthetic needs of civilized society, the reactions of science have so far been unfortunate. Its materialistic basis has directed attention to *things* as opposed to *values*. The antithesis is a false one, if taken in a concrete sense. But it is valid at the abstract level of ordinary thought. This misplaced emphasis coalesced with the abstractions of political economy, which are in fact the abstractions in terms of which commercial affairs are carried on. Thus all thought concerned with social organization expressed itself in terms of material things and of capital. Ultimate values were excluded. They were politely bowed to, and then handed over to the clergy to be kept for Sundays. A creed of competitive business morality was evolved, in some respects curiously high, but entirely devoid of consideration for the value of human life. The workmen were conceived a mere hands, drawn from the pool of labour. (*SMW* 202-03)

Whitehead was concerned primarily about the underdevelopment and undervaluation of our aesthetic needs, sensitivities, capacities, and creativity in his day, the 1920s (*SMW* 199-204), but things are probably even worse today. Even more serious both then and now is the corruption, underdevelopment, and undervaluation of our moral and spiritual needs, sensitivities, and capacities. Our whole souls are corrupted by the excessive attention given to and overvaluation of material or sensory objects by modern science, philosophy, and culture. Religion itself is so corrupted, Whitehead realized, for "Religion is tending to degenerate into a decent formula to embellish a comfortable life" (*SMW* 188).

ETHICAL DUTIES TO WHAT?

Despite Whitehead's "Morality emphasizes the detailed occasion" (*MT* 39), I agree with Brian Henning (156) that we have moral obligations only to enduring societies [or souls] but never to individual actual occasions as such. Transient occasions, he says, "perish no sooner than they are completed" and "it is not possible to affect them directly." How deeply into the great chain of becoming do our moral duties go? If we have no moral duties to actual occasions, do we have moral duties to electrons, protons, atoms, molecules, and living cells? We might have minimal direct ethical duties at times to some living cells and plants, but since "Life is robbery," as Whitehead said (*PR* 105), these duties seldom extend beyond minimizing harms and conflicts, becoming vegetarians, and cultivating a tragic sense of life.

How could we ever have any *direct* moral duties to lesser enduring societies like molecules, atoms, electrons, and other sub-atomic particles and waves—or to mere aggregates of them? If we could morally affect their well or ill being, our effects upon them would be too trivial to worry about, and innumerable competing macroscopic moral concerns (e.g., people and animals) are much more significant and make much stronger claims on our time and energy. Classical science was wrong in conceiving of molecules, atoms, and sub-atomic particles as vacuous actualities with nothing going on inside of them, and as having no value, self-significance, internal sensitivity, or evaluative responsiveness to their environment. Yet, there is very little if anything that we could ever actually do to affect the experience-quality of unconscious or barely conscious molecules, atoms, electrons, protons, etc.

In the very rare instances where we can directly affect them using powerful scientific devices, we do not know if they experience these effects positively or negatively. When we position electrons to dissolve into waves before going through two tiny slits, do they like it or dislike it? Does this help or hurt their well being? Are they thrilled or distressed? We really do not know. They are sensitive enough to their environment to realize in advance that they have to split in such circumstances, and they know when to do so, but do they really mind? When we "smash" atoms, do they care? Does it matter to an atom whether it is located in the statue of David or in just another old rock? Probably not. Besides, the very fact of observation seems to affect them, so we really don't know what they experience "behind our backs" when we are not looking, or whether they prefer an unobserved state to being observed. Quantum theory says that unobserved subatomic particles do not have the properties of observed particles, and vice versa. We have no sensory images in the mode of presentational immediacy that picture or reflect them. In themselves they may be nothing more than jittery vibrations, strings, or waves that aren't waving anything (*SMW* 35-37, 131-37; Edwards 2001, Ch. 6). Atomic theory is much more like poetry than like the "science" of the Logical Positivists' Principle of Verification. Empirically, today's "scientific" cosmology can hardly be distinguished from science fiction or blatant metaphysical speculation.

Clearly, all of our *direct* moral duties and concerns are to or with macroscopic or at least living cellular-level entities, not with or to non-living microscopic spatiotemporal objects, to anything's transient actual occasions, or to merely soul-less macroscopic aggregates—no matter how beautiful.

Whitehead said that "Each is all in all" (*PR* 348), and "Every actual entity is present in every other actual entity" (50). The interdependence of and our relations with everything else in the universe somehow make a difference. Quantum theory now confirms what Einstein called (and rejected as) "spooky action at a distance" at the sub-atomic level. This is now called "non-locality." Seldom noticed, however, Whitehead also affirmed that very often our relations to the rest of the universe make very *little* difference. Yes, "For each volume of space, or each lapse of time, includes in its essence aspects of all volumes of space, or all lapses of time" (*SMW* 71, 91); but too much emphasis on dependence is "an exaggeration of the community of the Universe," and "In any two occasions of the Universe there are elements in either one which are irrelevant to the constitution of the other" (*AI* 198). (The "butterfly effect" is a myth.) Whitehead thought that we should avoid "an over-moralization of things," and he concluded, "Fortunately there are a great many things which do not much matter, and we can have them how we will" (199). This is not as romantic as "Each is all in all," but it has a significant bearing on practical ethics. We have no moral duties to those we cannot significantly influence.

We have no direct moral duties to purely material macroscopic objects because they have no souls, no sakes of their own. We have no moral duties to individual actual occasions or to atomic and sub-atomic level particles and waves partly because we cannot influence them, partly because we do not know how to benefit or hurt them, and partly because they just do not much matter compared to so many other things that do matter. Usually if not always, our concerns and efforts can be better spent. Only unique, complex, enduring, conscious, macroscopic individuals matter morally. Only such individuals are moral agents, and only they have enough intrinsic worth to be of moral concern to us.

3.

THE GOOD AND THE BEAUTIFUL ETHICS VERSUS AESTHETICS

Intrinsic goodness is the most basic concept of ethics. We have direct moral duties only to intrinsically valuable entities; we have indirect moral duties to other things because they affect the well-being and continued existence of intrinsically valuable entities. If self-significant, conscious, enduring, unique individuals are intrinsically good, do only they have intrinsic worth, or do other values like beauty and creativity, so heavily emphasized in traditional process ethics, also have intrinsic worth? Philosophers have offered many answers other than "unique, conscious, enduring, valuing individuals" to the question, "What things are intrinsically good?" Some examples are: beauty, truth, knowledge, virtue, conscientiousness, desire fulfillment, interest fulfillment, pleasure, happiness, preference fulfillment, self-realization, etc. Something very important about such properties should be carefully noted. They are all repeatable universals, not unique individuals. They are "eternal objects," in Whitehead's vocabulary. They are not the individual actual entities into which these repeatable qualities may be concretely ingressed.

Several very serious ethical questions arise when any one or more universals is classified as intrinsically good. First, do they fulfill the defining characteristics of "intrinsically good"? Second, are only they but not unique individuals intrinsically good? Third, if only universals, not unique individuals, have intrinsic worth, what kind of value do we and the animals have as unique individuals? The answer to this last question must be:

only extrinsic worth. If only such universals are intrinsically good, then we as unique personal or animal souls are merely useful containers that hold all the good stuff, but otherwise we are worth nothing. We concrete, unique, conscious individuals are not the intrinsically good stuff on this view; only the universals or eternal objects within us are. We are merely useful receptacles, and that's it. But this conclusion is very hard to accept.

Hedonism well illustrates this predicament. If only pleasures are intrinsically good, then what is the value of the individual subjects experiencing the pleasures? The answer must be: They have only the instrumental significance of containers that hold the good stuff that really matters. Kantian ethics is in the same boat. When Kant explained what he really meant by "respecting persons as ends," this turned out to be nothing more than respecting the moral law within them. As he put it, "All respect for a person is only respect for the law (of righteousness, etc.) of which the person provides an example" (21 n). In other words, people are valuable only as containers for holding the moral law.

Our immediate problem is whether standard process ethics is in the same predicament. If only beauty or other repeatable aesthetic qualities are intrinsically good, then the real value of individual experiencing subjects is that of useful or extrinsically valuable buckets for holding beauty or other aesthetic qualities. In current process ethics, there is a serious ambiguity about beauty versus unique souls as intrinsically good. Brian Henning well illustrates this. On some pages, he seems to say or presuppose that beauty is the only intrinsic good (99-100, 125-26, 133-34, 149, 150-51) and that "importance and beauty are equivalent" (129, 151), but on other pages he affirms or presupposes the intrinsic worth of unique valuing individual subjects (143, 147, 159, 176, 178-79). His claim "that something is good or bad only if a particular individual feels it to be so" (142) is compatible with the view that individuals are valuable only as extrinsically useful vessels for holding and feeling the intrinsic goodness of beauty. Such ambiguities should be resolved in a viable process ethics.

IS BEAUTY INTRINSICALLY GOOD?

The "beauty versus individuals" dilemma never arises if beauty is not intrinsically good, so, let's begin with beauty, so heavily emphasized by Whitehead and most process ethicists. Is the universal, beauty, intrinsically good? Does "beauty" fulfill the defining characteristics of "intrinsically good"? Going further, are "good" and "beautiful" synonyms, or equivalent in meaning? What about other universal aesthetic or non-aesthetic values? Charles Hartshorne acknowledged, "Though beauty is the ideal aesthetic value, it is not the only one" (1970, 304). Deviations from beauty are also aesthetic values, as explained in Hartshorne's aesthetic circle (305). He recognized many additional aesthetic concepts and values—"Neat," "Ugly," Magnificent," "Sublime," "Tragic," "Commonplace," "Pretty," and "Ridiculous." He understood all of these to be deviations from "Beautiful," so beauty is axiologically basic. Not all aestheticians would agree, and some might add additional aesthetic concepts, but that is beyond our present concerns.

Are beauty and intrinsic goodness the same? A clear answer is hard to get from Whitehead himself. Hartshorne equated intrinsic goodness with "aesthetic value," understood more broadly than "beauty." He wrote, "Since the intrinsic value of experiences is by definition aesthetic value, and since goodness is the disinterested will to enhance the value of future experiences, ethics presupposes aesthetics" (1970, 308). John Cobb clearly identified intrinsic goodness with beauty. Speaking for both Whitehead and himself, he thought, "Whitehead has chosen beauty as the clue to what is finally worthwhile in itself... Beauty is the only intrinsic value" (1965, 104), and "We will assume here the understanding of intrinsic value as strength of beauty developed above" (122, 108). Cobb's emphasis on "strength" was absorbed into the very meaning of "beauty" in Hartshorne's aesthetic circle, where weak beauty counts as "pretty" but not as beauty itself.

Perhaps Whitehead understood that beauty means nothing to itself, that it has no self-significance. Nevertheless, beauty was his primary value, though he never explicitly categorized it as intrinsically good. "The world is good only when it is beautiful" (*AI* 268), he wrote, and that is about as close as he came. He said much more about beauty and other aesthetic topics than about the intrinsic worth of individuals. He often subordinated ethics to aesthetics, but I have not caught him explicitly identifying intrinsic goodness with beauty. Nevertheless, this would be in harmony with the fundamental status he gave to both aesthetics and beauty. Most process ethicists affirm that aesthetics takes precedence over ethics, indeed that aesthetics is the essence of ethics itself (Henning 125-35). An important exception to this was Lynne Belaief, who regarded Whitehead's equating of ethics with aesthetics as "only apparent" and "intentionally metaphorical" (50-53), and who viewed the intrinsic value of self-identical individuals as axiologically fundamental (53-56, 67-94, 110-11, 139, 163). She never got beyond treating individual souls as societies of actual occasions, but this book argues that she was right in ranking concrete persons and animals over beauty.

Clearly, for some process thinkers, making aesthetics fundamental is the same thing as making beauty both axiologically fundamental and identical with intrinsic goodness. Whiteheadian morality aims at maximizing "importance" (*MT* 13-14), and this can be construed as the maximization of beauty (Henning 129, 133-34). Many process philosophers who support the idea that aesthetics is more fundamental than ethics also proclaim that the very aim or purpose of God in creation is the creation of beauty (Henning 129; Griffin 2000, 293, 300; Cobb 1965, 180).

I strongly object to all of this and wish to reverse all process propensities to treat ethics as a species of aesthetics, and beauty as intrinsically good. Here are my reasons.

BEAUTY FAILS THE TEST

First, *beauty* does not fulfill Whitehead's own definition of "intrinsically good," as this was developed in Chapter Two. Beauty, by any definition, is not a self or other valuing, conscious, enduring, unique individual. It is not an individual actual occasion or entity. It is not an enduring society of actual occasions. It is not a unique, conscious, partly self perpetuating and self valuing field. It is not God, who is a single absolutely unique everlasting, constantly concrescing actual entity with personal attributes. Treating beauty as fundamental violates Whitehead's own "ontological principle," which says, "No actual entity, no reason" (*PR* 19) and "Actual entities are the only reasons" (24). This should apply just as much to process ethics as to its metaphysics. Unique enduring souls as actual entities might count as finally real reasons in ethics, but not beauty. Beauty in itself is a universal, an eternal object, originally only a mere possibility in the Primordial Nature of God. Even when concretely ingressed within us or in the rest of creation, it is still a complex eternal object, a universal, not an actual entity. Beauty clearly isn't a fundamental reality or actuality in process metaphysics, and "no actual entity, no reason" should imply that it is not axiologically fundamental.

Hartman defined "beauty" as "aesthetic 'good'" (1967, 180), but he did very little to elaborate on this. He defined "aesthetics" as "the application of intrinsic value to individual things" (114), though the scope of aesthetics is probably wider than that. Process thinkers do better. What is the process definition of "beauty"? Brian Henning (102, 100-12) does a marvelous job explaining Charles Hartshorne's aesthetic circle and his understanding of "beauty" as "unity in variety" (1970, 303-04). "Unity, diversity, complexity, and simplicity" are basic definitional beauty-making properties, as Henning masterfully explains (107). Anything that exemplifies the right proportions of those universal properties is beautiful. Beauty is a delicate adjustment and combination of such universals. As any of them diminish, beauty wanes in a variety of aesthetic ways.

Beauty is an abstract value composition, a complex set of universals or eternal objects. It is what Whitehead called "an eternal object 'complex,'" made up of "component eternal objects" (*SMW* 166). This value combination may ingress concretely into actualized individuals and groups, but beauty itself is not a self-experiencing, conscious, valuing, actual entity. Actual entities have power and mean something to themselves. As Whitehead said, "An entity is actual, when it has significance for itself" (*PR* 25). Eternal objects are only formal but not efficient causes. They exist, function, and have value only for and within actual entities. So it is with beauty.

Process ethics says that we should strive to produce lives for ourselves and others that are as beautiful as possible, lives and social orders that exhibit the right proportions of unity, diversity, complexity, and simplicity. There is nothing at all wrong with this ideal of creating as much beauty or unity in variety as possible, given the qualification that beauty is for our sake, not for its own sake. Although Whitehead once wrote of "aesthetic worth for its own sake" (*MT* 119), beauty does not exist for itself because it has no sake and is no self. Only unique, experiencing, valuing, individual actualities have a sake. Having a sake means being a soul or subject who fulfills the five defining conditions of intrinsic value explained previously. If, as Whitehead thought, being intrinsically good consists most fundamentally in having significance to self, that is, in valuing self or others, then beauty could not possibly be intrinsically good. Beauty, like material aggregates, is not itself a unique, experiencing, valuing actual occasion or entity, not even when ingressed into actualities. Beauty has great significance to and for us, as does the car in our garage, but neither beauty nor the car has significance for itself, cares for others, or values the universe. Neither one knows that it is beautiful. Neither one knows anything. Neither values anything. Neither one cares. Neither one is a conscious evaluative self or soul, so neither could ever have any value to or for itself.

Many objective physical conditions of beauty exist outside of us, but experienced or subjective beauty literally exists, not as an actual experiencing subject itself, but "only in the eye of the beholder." The ultimate beholder is God, but we are lesser beholders. In his favor, Whitehead occasionally came very close to making both beauty and the individuals who experience it essential features of process ethics.

> Now there are two sides to aesthetic experience. In the first place, it involves a subjective sense of individuality. It is *my* enjoyment. I may forget myself; but all the time the enjoyment is mine, the pleasure is mine, and the pain is mine. Aesthetic enjoyment demands an individualized universe. (*SP* 139)

"Mine" here seems to refer to my enduring individuality, not to actual occasions. Morality, Whitehead thought, aims at the maximization of "importance," (*MT* 13-14), by which he meant goodness or value. In this respect, his moral outlook closely resembles classical Utilitarian morality, which aims at "the greatest happiness of the greatest number." Here, for Whitehead, the enjoyment is *for* individuals. Yet, beauty rather than pleasure was his most basic value concept, with only occasional ambivalent allusions to individuals.

Whitehead recognized that at times we do immoral things that minimize or destroy value or importance. But he simply muddied the waters when he wrote, "The destruction of a man, or of an insect, or of a tree, or of the Parthenon may be moral or immoral" (*MT* 14). His main point was that destroying good things is justified occasionally for the sake of saving or creating even better things. Here he also affirmed the positive value of people, insects, trees, and beautiful buildings like the Parthenon, but why is the Parthenon included in this list? Do all of these items have intrinsic importance as self or other valuing actualities? Lumping them all together only creates confusion when read in light of, "Everything has some value for itself, for others, and for the whole" (*MT* 111).

BEAUTIFUL AGGREGATES

The concept of "vacuous actualities" should be allowed an honored place in process ethics. Many experientially prominent things, macroscopic perceptual aggregates, have great value for others and perhaps for the whole, but not for themselves. Their value is instrumental, not intrinsic. What kind of value or "importance" do people, insects, trees, and beautiful buildings actually have? Do they all have equal value? The same kind of value? If intrinsic value involves having significance in, to, and for oneself, everyday people, cows, maybe insects, perhaps even some trees, and even individual cells—including microbes or unicellular living things—probably have that, but beautiful buildings like the Parthenon do not. As macroscopic perceptual wholes, beautiful buildings, cars, clothes, TV sets, jewels, "precious metals," physical works of art, and other material objects have no self-significance because they have no selves.

The Parthenon is no doubt a very beautiful building that has immense aesthetic and historical significance for us, but it has none whatsoever to or for itself. The beauty of the macroscopic Parthenon is *for us,* not *for itself,* because it has no self, no soul, no experience, no consciousness, no values. Like any old rock or a hunk of steel, it actually is a merely mindless thing. For all practical and ethical intents and purposes, it really is a vacuous actuality. Its atoms and molecules may have minute self-significance, but not the Parthenon itself. Considered as a macroscopic whole, its value is purely instrumental. Its beauty, harmony, usefulness, and importance are for us. Many things that are very good for us are not good or important to, within, and for themselves.

If we have any moral duties to the Parthenon, for example to preserve it as best we can, and not bulldoze it away, they are not *direct* duties to the instrumentally valuable Parthenon. No matter how beautiful and historically significant, the Parthenon is only extrinsically good or useful to us. It is not intrinsically good or valuable to, in, and for itself. This is just as true of the world's greatest paintings and sculptures as of the Parthenon, though we are often so overwhelmed by lovely and sublime aesthetic objects that we mistakenly attribute intrinsic worth to them. G.E. Moore's exquisitely beautiful world that no one (no sentient, living, human, or Divine being) ever experiences has no intrinsic worth, and even he eventually came to that conclusion. Not just worldly people but highly sophisticated human aesthetes often attribute intrinsic worth to mere things because they are beautiful to us.

Our moral duties to the Parthenon and other great works of art are only *indirect* duties to them, because of their *direct* effects on human beings, but great works of art know nothing of and care nothing for us or for themselves. Still, they have great significance to us; they are very good for us. Their grand beauty and continued existence contribute immensely to our human well-being. Brian Henning suggests that we should not treat the Parthenon as having "purely instrumental value" (147), which seems to imply that we have direct moral duties to it; but since "it has no 'sake of its own,'" (his words) he should assign only the same instrumental value to it that he does to a beautiful boulder, rock, or some other aggregate (157).

Like every other good thing, beauty can be overvalued, undervalued, or mistaken for some other kind of value. Whitehead complained that scientific materialism's "bare valuelessness of matter led to a lack of reverence in the treatment of natural or artistic beauty" (*SMW* 196). True enough, but dogmatic materialism is also just as much a threat to moral values and to the values of reason, logic, and science. Panexperientialism, by contrast, helps both to resolve the metaphysical mind/body problem and to understand our indirect ethical relations with soul-less aggregates. Materialism's "lack of reverence" for beauty resulted primarily from its denial that unique *people* have souls, not from its denial that beautiful inanimate macroscopic *things* have souls—because they really don't have souls. On process grounds, in themselves the Parthenon, the Mona Lisa, and the statue of David are mere aggregates. No souls of Athena, Mona Lisa, or David are in them. No great works of art have their own souls, their own intensely conscious, dominant, enduring, valuing, self-significant actualities. In themselves, they are just physically structured elements, molecules, and atoms. Beauty cannot be good *for the soul* where there is no soul; beauty cannot be good for itself for it has no soul. Whitehead got it right when he wrote, "Great art is the arrangement of the environment so as to provide for the soul vivid, but transient, values" (*SMW* 202, italics added). Beauty has immense instrumental worth for us, but it should not be so overvalued that we attribute intrinsic value to it.

WELL-BEING, GOOD FOR, AND INTRINSICALLY GOOD

Overall well-being must be distinguished from intrinsic goodness. To be intrinsically good, valuable for its own sake, an entity must have certain minimal properties. It must be self or other valuing, conscious, enduring, individuated, and unique. Sadly, many intrinsically valuable persons and animals do not have very much well-being, for this requires many additional good-making properties. Many people and animals are "bad off," as we sometimes say. The good-making properties of well-being or abundant living go far beyond the five properties that define intrinsic goodness. Some of these additional properties will be identified next. They will be called *"intrinsic value enhancers" or "good for" properties.*

My third and most important reason for not reducing ethics to aesthetics is that we should not confuse being *good for* something with being *intrinsically good,* even when the "good for" properties exist only within us. Many if not most philosophers have been confused about this, and I suspect that Whitehead himself was. A is "good for" B if A enriches or enhances the overall well-being of B, that is, if the combination of A with B benefits B. Consider value combinations where A is an intrinsically valuable enduring individual, but B is only a universal that is good for A. By no means is "good for" identical with "being an end in itself" or "being of value to or for itself." "Good for" values have no significance to themselves, for they are not selves. A-type entities such as people, animals, and other enduring self-significant individuals are of value in, to, and for themselves, but B-type universals, beauty and pleasure for example, are of value only because they are good for some A, only because they benefit some A, only because some A's life-experience or overall well-being is enriched by B, though the B will never know it or care. The B-type entities we are now discussing can exist only within A-type entities.

In one sense, all *external* extrinsic or instrumental sensory goods like pure water, clean air, material prosperity, and beautiful physical aggregates (e.g., sunsets, paintings, and mansions) are good for us. They are of benefit to us, but *they exist initially outside of us* before any of their properties enter into us perceptually. They have no significance to or for themselves. They do not value themselves, us, or anything. They become of value only when they are valued by us, and we can evaluate them in many different ways—in three dimensions, as explained in the next chapter.

There is a distinctive class of "good for us" values that can and do *exist only within or inside of us*. These are "intrinsic value enhancers." These internal value-objects never exist external to our conscious minds or souls, but they still have no significance to themselves, for they are not or have not selves or valuing subjects. They contribute directly to our well-being, but they exist *only within* our conscious minds or souls. We are directly and experientially acquainted with them only internally, introspectively, or in the Whiteheadian perceptual mode of causal efficacy. Prime examples are curiosity, knowledge, truth, creativity, pleasures, moral conscientiousness, desire satisfaction, and experienced beauty.

The main reason why so many philosophers have confused such "good for us" properties with intrinsic goods is that they can and do exist only within unique, conscious, valuing subjects like us, and we usually identify ourselves very closely with them. That they are not subjects and have no significance to themselves is easily overlooked, even by process thinkers. Another reason for the confusion is that one of them is enjoyment itself, and the others are inherently and immediately enjoyable. To the extent that pleasure is "its own reward," agreeable feelings and processes are easily confused with intrinsic goods. But whose reward is pleasure? Not its own. Many such soul-less "good for us" properties lack self-significance and exist only within individual actual entities like us. Several examples emphasized by process thinkers will now be discussed.

PLEASURES AND HAPPINESS

Experienced beauty is not the only no-self property that is *good for* us and other animals, and it is not the only one that has been confused with *intrinsic goodness*. Another striking example of this is *pleasure, happiness, enjoyment, or affective satisfaction*. Hedonists claim that only pleasure has intrinsic value. The truth is, pleasure is not valuable in, to, or for itself; it is valuable only in, to, and for us, the animals, and other sentient or experiencing realities. Pleasure is good for us and valuable for our sake, not for its own.

Whitehead clearly valued enjoyment, especially "self-enjoyment." In one of his many variations on the aim of creation, "The aim is at that complex of feeling which is the enjoyment of those data in that way. 'That way of enjoyment' is selected from the boundless wealth of alternatives," and "The aim is at the enjoyment belonging to the process" (*MT* 152). *Happiness* is hedonically defined as prolonged pleasure, enjoyment, or agreeable feeling with little or no pain. Hedonists say that pleasure itself, or happiness so understood, is the only thing that is valuable for its own sake; it is the only thing that is intrinsically good. Some thought that "intrinsically good" just means "pleasant"—a clear instance of the "naturalistic fallacy" discussed in the next chapter.

John Stuart Mill astutely discerned that "pleasure" refers to many different qualities of agreeable feeling, not just to one (Edwards, 1979, Chs. 1 and 2). The agreeable feelings derived from listening to Mozart or Bach, or from reading a great novel, or from loving a baby, are qualitatively different from the agreeable feelings derived from eating and drinking. Whitehead himself recognized, "There are qualitative differences between different types of happiness" (*AI* 40). We can agree with Mill's insightful psychology of pleasure and pain while not accepting (as I once did) his theory that qualitatively distinct pleasures, and they alone, are intrinsically good. People, not pleasures or enjoyment, have intrinsic worth. My own exposure to Hartmanian axiology eventually convinced me of that. Unique souls have more than merely instrumental worth as useful containers for holding qualitatively distinct pleasures. Still, pleasure is very desirable because it is good for us.

"Happiness" is not necessarily hedonic in meaning. There are pluralistic or eudemonistic definitions of "happiness" that view sustained pleasure as just one intrinsic good among others. A plurality of universals are intrinsically good on this view, and together they constitute happiness. The ingredients of eudemonistic "happiness" could be any combination of things like beauty, truth, knowledge, creativity, conscientiousness, virtue, desire fulfillment, interest fulfillment, pleasure, preference fulfillment, self-realization, etc. Even this pluralistic or eudemonistic view of happiness mistakenly attributes intrinsic worth to universals, not unique individuals.

For the moment, we are concerned with hedonic happiness understood as sustained pleasure or enjoyment with few or no pains. Pleasures or enjoyments, even if qualitatively many, and even when concretely ingressed into and sustained within unique conscious actualities, are abstractions, universals, *eternal objects*. They are not concretely existing, psychophysical, unique *actualities with self-significance*. They are not capable of valuing themselves and others. Pleasures, though qualitatively diverse, are not souls, or selves, or conscious, or self-conscious, or self or other valuing. Thus, pleasure, like both the Parthenon and beauty, has no sake, no self, no "to, for, or in itself." Hedonic happiness or enjoyment is very *good for* us and for other unique sentient or experiencing psychophysical enduring individuals, but it has no value at all "in itself" or "to itself," that is, when isolated in experience, thought, and imagination from concretely existing self-significant enduring subjects. Indeed, isolated from unique experiencing souls, it could not even exist, much less have value in, to, and for itself. Neither pleasure, nor happiness, nor any of the great "good for" universals discussed in this chapter can exist or have any worth at all in, to, or for themselves, that is, in isolation from us and other valuing subjects. Happiness is very good for us, but it should not be overvalued.

SATISFACTIONS

Whitehead had a great deal to say about *"satisfaction."* When reading him we are always tempted to give the word its ordinary valuational meaning rather than his own purely technical metaphysical meaning. Sometimes this works, sometimes not. Ordinarily, "satisfaction" means internally experienced pleasure, enjoyment, happiness, or agreeable feeling, which is usually good for us and has positive axiological significance. This is the very stuff of which hedonic happiness is made, as just noted. When we get satisfaction from a good meal, from a good book, from philosophical thinking, or from sex, this means that we really enjoy it. When victims get satisfaction in court, this means that they take vindictive pleasure in the punishment of offenders, especially their own victimizers. Sometimes "satisfaction" just means "enjoyable desire-fulfillment," as when our desires or interests are fulfilled, giving us pleasure. When our desires are fulfilled we tend to be satisfied in the sense of pleased. Hartshorne had this ordinary sense of "satisfaction" in mind when he wrote of "the very meaning of good, which is satisfaction, fruition of purpose enjoyed by the purposer" (1948, 130). G.E. Moore, of course, would have recognized this as another clear instance of the "naturalistic fallacy."

Whitehead used "satisfaction" in its ordinary hedonic sense of "pleasurable satisfaction" (*SP* 109) occasionally (*FR* 8, *AI* 11, 46, 67, 70, 172, 291; *MT* 122, and *perhaps PR* 111-12), but most of his very prolific discussions of "satisfaction" are completely metaphysical, not axiological. His metaphysical satisfactions are value-neutral in the sense that they apply just as much to evil as to goodness, just as much to excruciating pains as to great pleasures. When his actual occasions achieve metaphysical satisfaction, this means *only* that they arrive at *definiteness and completion* before perishing (*PR* 26, 84-87, 219-220, 292-93). Actual occasions do have aims and feelings, including self or other enjoyments, but these belong to the earlier phases of concrescence, and by satisfaction-time, they are finished.

Whitehead's metaphysical "satisfaction" differs significantly from internally experienced pleasures, enjoyment, happiness, desire-fulfillment, self-realization, goodness, or positive value of any kind, though some process thinkers may assume that they are the same (e.g., Gray 43-73; Belaief 80-83, 97, 160, 166). James R. Gray's view was that "Process ethics is based upon the aim at maximal satisfaction" (62), and "Pleasure and harmony [beauty] can be understood to have the exact same meaning" (31). John Goheen clearly confused the two senses of satisfaction (455-58), especially when he objected, "Presumably indefinite pattern is as much a source of satisfaction as 'definite pattern' or 'unity'" (458). By "satisfaction" he meant agreeable feelings, but every actual occasion achieves satisfaction in the sense of definiteness.

Associating positive hedonic meaning with Whitehead's metaphysical sense of "satisfaction" may be quite commonplace among process thinkers. Yet, as he *defined* it, "satisfaction" is purely metaphysical, not evaluative. Sheer definiteness and completion may themselves function as highly abstract values, but Whitehead's metaphysical satisfactions are otherwise axiologically neutral. They fall equally upon the just and the unjust, the happy and the unhappy, the good and the bad, the beautiful and the ugly. The most excruciatingly painful and desire-frustrating experiences fully achieve Whiteheadian satisfaction (definiteness and completion), as do the most morally abhorrent behaviors and the most aesthetically repulsive circumstances. Everything that happened in Hitler's concentration camps achieved perfect Whiteheadian satisfaction. Massive evil is just as fully determinate and complete as massive goodness. Fortunately, it too passes away. As traditionally understood, without passing away, Hell is just as fully determinate and complete as

Heaven—and just as deep or intense in feelings. Thus, beyond fleeting determinateness and completion, sometimes utterly horrible, we cannot say that Whiteheadian metaphysical satisfaction is good for us here and now, and it is certainly not good in or to itself, for it is an abstraction, not a self. Pleasure and beauty may be good for us, but not sheer definiteness and completion, which can be either bad or good for us. Often they are bad for us, for we deeply regret the transience of definite goodness, but we are glad for the transience of definite evils.

Definiteness and completion, the two defining characteristics of Whitehead's "satisfaction," *can be separated* from one another. This is essential in understanding Whitehead's God, who is an everlasting, single but constantly processing actual entity (Edwards, 2013a). God experiences the succession of created occasions, but God is not composed of actual occasions. As Whitehead said, "The term 'actual occasion' will always exclude God from its scope" (*PR* 88). God processes and concresces everlastingly and never perishes, so God never reaches satisfaction in the sense of *completion,* but God continuously achieves satisfaction in the sense of *definiteness.*

God also achieves satisfaction in the sense of *enjoyment.* God's inability to achieve Whiteheadian metaphysical satisfaction (as completion) also does not in any way interfere with God's capacity to achieve satisfaction as we *ordinarily* understand the term. God can and does constantly experience the full definiteness of pleasure, enjoyment, happiness, desire-fulfillment, self-realization, beauty, intrinsic goodness, and positive values of every kind. According to Whitehead, "No actual entity can be conscious of its own satisfaction" (*PR* 85), i.e., their own completion, presumably; but this does not mean that actual occasions or entities cannot be conscious of their own enjoyments or satisfactions as ordinarily understood. We can be and are conscious of ours, and God is conscious of all created joys and delights, and of his own enjoyment of them. Happiness is very good for us and very good for God, but it should not be overvalued.

God also suffers from every evil inflicted on every creature in its full definiteness, finality, anguish, and loss. God loves, delights in, and identifies with (intrinsically evaluates) all creatures, all subjects who endure, as well as with their transient experiences of all that is good for them. Whitehead's compassionate God feels our pain as well as our pleasure. As he said, God is our "fellow sufferer who understands" (PR 351).

Once both definite and completed, *perishing actual occasions* become instrumental goods, superjective, useful to others (85), but no longer valuable to themselves. *Determinate enduring (non-perishing) actual entities or souls* can be and are valuable to themselves in ways other than finality or completeness. Satisfaction as both determinateness and terminal completion can and must be separated in God and in determinate enduring human and animal souls.

As single and relatively enduring actual entities constantly achieving definiteness and absorbing successive actual occasions, we are shadows and images of God. As enduring soul-fields, we, like God, do not perish ontologically every fraction of a second. Our total reality now includes all of our past and present successive occasions of experience. These have perished to themselves but not within our total property inventory. Unlike God we are never fully aware of who we really are, that is, of the full richness of our own properties. Past occasions are still active in the present only to the extent that they continue to influence and are preserved within our relatively enduring souls. Our memories are woefully incomplete, unlike God's. God as an enduring actual entity can experience succession without perishing, and without being composed only of actual occasions. So can we. God constantly experiences and immortalizes the succession of events in the world without perishing himself as an actual entity. Like God, as enduring soul-fields, we experience succession without perishing every fraction of a second, but our experiences do perish into the past. So do most of our memories. Yet, our forgotten experiences, very broadly understood, remain as parts of who we are, of our total property inventories as unique individuals.

To the worry that conceiving of God as an everlasting single continuously concrescing and never completed actual entity makes God an exception to all metaphysical principles, the obvious reply is that this assumes that all other contingent metaphysical realities are fleeting actual occasions. However, if single, relatively enduring, continuously concrescing, uncompleted soul fields flood the universe, God exemplifies all basic metaphysical principles and is no exception.

CREATIVITY

Creativity, choosing, and acting from choice are universal human properties that contribute to our overall intrinsic goodness and well-being. All human beings are creative, make free choices, and act upon them. Some people are much more creative and make more momentous decisions with more consequential effects than others. We regularly make creative choices in dealing with the ordinary affairs of life and in relating to others. There is some ordinariness even about outstandingly creative artists, musicians, writers, thinkers, philosophers, inventors, social engineers, and moral activists. All of us are partly self-creative, and our self-originated choices, efforts, initiatives, and actions influence human, animal, and environmental others by degrees. All of us are responsible for the decisions we make, for the voluntary control we exercise over what we think, how we feel, what we do, and for their immediate and long-range consequences. Many of us are immensely creative and concentrate intensely on what we are creating (works of art, systems of thought, ethical theories, practical inventions, or better social conditions and relations), and we intensely identify ourselves with our creations during our most innovative moments. Through self-creativity we partly fulfill our ideal self-concepts.

Creativity is an important theme and value in process thought. It is usually associated with aesthetics rather than with ethics, even though one can be creative in many ways, including morally and spiritually. But what kind of reality does creativity have, and exactly what kind of value does it have? Prompted by Whitehead's own treatment of creativity as the "Category of the Ultimate" and "the universal of universals" (*PR* 21-22), some process thinkers seem almost to give it a "finally real" status of its own. Some treat it as a metaphysical necessity, something "equally primordial" with God (Griffin, 1989, 41)—as if it were a power that exists and functions along with and independently of God and created individuals. As David Griffin put it, "Whitehead and Hartshorne do not simply equate God with creativity but regard creativity as the ultimate reality which is embodied by both God and all worldly individuals" (38). On this view, God is subject to its independent power and necessarily exemplifies it. Creativity has power over God; God does not have power over it. Creativity is ultimate; God is not.

Part of the problem here is that if creativity is treated as a necessarily existing power that functions along with and independently of God and created individuals, this violates Whitehead's own ontological principle, according to which only concrete actualities are finally real and efficacious. Creativity was not ontologically fundamental for Whitehead himself. It depends on God and creatures, for "there is no meaning to 'creativity' apart from its 'creatures' (*PR* 225). It is a "universal," Whitehead's own word for it (21), and "without a character of its own" (31). Obviously, creativity is not a self-significant concrete individual or actuality. To regard it as such commits Whitehead's "fallacy of misplaced concreteness," the fallacy of "mistaking the abstract for the concrete" (*SMW* 51), the fallacy of reifying abstractions or universals as if they were individual actualities and agents.

Many supporters of today's "open theology" or "relational theology" strongly object to giving independent *metaphysical* actuality, necessity, and power to creativity, and to making it ultimate over God. They are temporalistic theologians who agree that God experiences temporal change, but they distance themselves from process theologians like Griffin. They think it better to treat creativity as a perfect-making *moral* attribute of God than as a *metaphysical necessity*. Creativity, they hold, is a moral aspect of God's overall goodness, and it is at God's disposal and within God's control. It is not an independent metaphysical reality. If God is necessarily creative, this is because of God's own internal love and self-giving moral goodness. Creating is a moral necessity for a loving God, not a metaphysical necessity imposed on God "from the outside" (Oord 125). God does not depend on creativity; creativity depends on God. For what it is worth, I agree.

According to Griffin, Whitehead's decree that God is the "chief exemplification (*PR* 343) of all metaphysical principles, including creativity, means that "the ultimate creativity of the universe is necessarily embodied in finite actualities as well as in the divine actuality" (Griffin 2000, 93, 96). Many temporalistic theologians do not call themselves process theologians because they profoundly believe that some moral and spiritual insights and values override Whitehead's metaphysical decrees. There is a necessity about creation, they think, but it is moral rather than metaphysical. Our values have a significant bearing on how we conceive of God, and we may honestly disagree about the perfect-making qualities or attributes of *that being than whom none richer in perfect-making properties can be conceived.* Process theologians disagree with classical theologians about this, and both process and temporalistic theists may disagree among themselves. It all depends on what we value most.

The other problem about creativity is the tendency, or at least the temptation, to view it as having intrinsic value, but it does not. Creativity is not ontologically fundamental, and it is not axiologically fundamental. Creativity, like pleasure, is only an abstraction, a universal, both as a mere possibility (an eternal object) and when instantiated or ingressed within concrete, conscious, self-significant individuals. Creativity is another "good for" value, but it has no sake, no self, no "mind of its own," so to speak. It is not an individual agent, it knows nothing, it has no value to itself, and it attaches no value to others; thus, it has no intrinsic goodness. It is very good for us and other creatures, and very good for God, but not good in, to, and for itself. It is essential for our own well-being and God's, but it should not be overvalued. Both creative change and sustainable stability in proper balance are good for us and for God.

TRUTH, KNOWLEDGE, BELIEFS, CONCEPTS

Merely soul-less *things* are the supreme values of practical "worldly" people, and they tend to love them "for their own sake." Many very different people value soul-less *intellectual or cognitive goods* for their own sake. Intellectuals, philosophers, theologians, scientists, college professors, authoritarians, and religious dogmatists are particularly tempted to thus value formalities, ideas, doctrines, knowledge, truths, rules, regulations, and beliefs. As John Cobb explained, scholars working in research universities claim to be "value free," (2010, 89) but at the same time "The university context does not support any other rationale than the goodness of knowledge for its own sake" (97). Valuing knowledge for its own sake is not value free!

Here we have exactly the same problem as with worldly materialistic values, pleasures, and beauty. Just as a macroscopic diamond ring has no sake, even so, purely systemic conceptual values have no sake, souls, self-awareness, or self or other evaluations. Intellectual goods have their own distinctive kind of value, systemic value, but not intrinsic value. As Hartshorne discerned, "Abstractions do not feel or think, not even the abstraction 'feeling' or 'thinking'" (1970, 141), and "The abstractions of metaphysics are not chiefly ends in themselves, but means to wisdom and goodness in the enjoyment and creation of the concrete" (119).

Even Kant's "moral law" has no "for its own sake," despite Kant's doting over it, for it too is mere abstraction that means nothing to itself. The law was made for us, for our well-being, not us for the law. Conceptual values are good for us, but not to, for, or in themselves. Many intellectuals get it backwards; they rank the systemic over the intrinsic. This goes hand in hand with loving the law, truth, knowledge, and abstractions more than people. Intellectual goods are often valued for their own sake, but they have no sake. Theologians also get it backwards when they rank first and foremost faith as cognitive assent to doctrines, beliefs, principles, and the books that contain them. Bibliolatry is a conspicuous form of both idolatry and axiological confusion. We are to love God first, then people—but not doctrines, truths, beliefs, and Good Books—with all our hearts, souls, minds, and strengths. Such systemic values may be good for us, but they are definitely not good in, to, and for themselves. They enhance our well-being, but they should not be overvalued, or valued over us and Godself.

SELF-REALIZATION

Self-realization of the unique enduring self is axiologically significant. Being a self takes time; realizing or becoming a self takes time. We desire to be informed, authentic, and integrated persons free from ignorance and conflicting interests, desires, and goals; but achieving informed, authentic, integrated selfhood also takes considerable time. We plan ahead, develop our talents, learn our lessons, pursue our careers, raise our children, prepare for retirement, etc., as if doing so for *ourselves,* as well as for others. We do not believe we are doing this merely for future actual occasions. Intrinsic evaluation of ourselves involves a prolonged, intense, positive axiological orientation toward our enduring futures, as well as toward our pasts and our present.

Many of the most important self-realization goods of life exist only *inside of us* and have the same axiological status as beauty, pleasure, and knowledge. *They are good for us, essential for our well-being, but not good in, to, or for themselves.* They can and do exist only intra-mentally, only within us. They are not perceptual objects existing first in our common, public, sensory world. Unlike single actual occasions, all of them are relatively enduring qualities, properties, or concretely ingressed eternal objects. They are valuable, not for their own sakes, only for our sakes.

Almost everything we seriously value, both individuals and everything "good for" them, persist for some period of time and do not perish every tenth of a second. *Even in a process universe, we only value things that endure.* Reason, intelligence, truth, and knowledge are good for us. Remembering the past is good for us. Choosing and acting for the future are good for us. Moral and aesthetic creativity and sensitivity are good for us. Adventure, spontaneity, zest, and novel experiences are good for us. Consciousness is good for us. Self-consciousness is good for us. Self-knowledge, self-concern, and self-respect are good for us. Knowledge of and concern for others are good for us. Happiness as diverse agreeable feelings and affections is good for us. Love and compassion are good for us (and obviously also for others affected by us). Moral virtues are good for us (and for others affected). Delight in the well-being and moral goodness of others is good for us. Practicing what we preach is good for us (and others). Moral and spiritual growth are good for us. Sensing and practicing the presence of God are good for us. Having values, i.e., evaluating, is good for us. Our positive individuating properties, the ones no one else has, are good for us. The purely internal beauty of personal existence is good for us, as is an awareness of the infinite beauty of God. This could go on and on, but we can summarily include all internally existing "good for" properties under the concept of *"self-realization."* All of the preceding positive universal properties are self-fulfilling. Self-realization is good for us. Our overall well-being is a synthesis of ourselves as enduring actual entities with our ongoing self-realization. Self-realization takes time. "Good for" properties are the good-making properties of self-realization and well-being. All of these fit into the Form of the Good.

Plausible lists of internal good-making properties inherent in well-being and self-realization could go on indefinitely, but all such very good things should be classified as "good for" rather than as "intrinsically good." Experienced beauty is one of those things. Its external conditions may exist objectively in the real world, like the external beauty of the structure of the Parthenon, the splendid glory of the purely physical aspects of the Grand Canyon, and the chemical and physical properties of the starry heavens above, but these mean nothing unless we experience them internally. Internally experienced beauties and harmonies are intrinsic value enhancers. They are only "good for" values having great significance to us, but none to themselves. Only constantly growing, enduring, self-significant, and self-actualizing selves, souls, or unique conscious individuals are intrinsically good. Thus, ethics is metaphysically, logically, and axiologically more fundamental than aesthetics. Echoing one version of Kant's ethical imperative, our most fundamental ethical obligation is to treat all unique, conscious, valuing individuals, (not just human beings,) as ends in themselves and never merely as means. Yet, in a world of conflict, woe, and tragedy, "merely as means" is often unavoidable. "Life is robbery," as Whitehead said (*PR* 105), but ethically we should strive to minimize robbery, conflict, and loss. We should seek the lesser of evils when there is no other choice and when robbery is inevitable.

THE PURPOSE OF THE UNIVERSE: INTENSITIES, OR BEAUTY

Whitehead expressed his understanding of "the purpose of the universe" in many different and not obviously coherent ways. In *Adventures of Ideas* (265), without mentioning God, but perhaps with God is mind, Whitehead said, "The teleology of the universe is directed to the production of Beauty." There are many difficulties with beauty, as previously explained. In *Religion in the Making*, he gave a more general and perhaps more acceptable statement of God's purpose: "The purpose of God is the attainment of value in the temporal world" (100). Unfortunately, after a few pages, he seemed to identify all value, including moral value, with aesthetic value (105), but we should not take this step with him. He identified God's purpose for the world in a number of different ways, as follows.

GOD'S PURPOSE AS THE INTENSIFICATION OF FEELING

In *Process and Reality,* Whitehead affirmed that "God's purpose in the creative advance is the evocation of intensities" (105), specifically "maximum depth of intensity of feeling" for every actual occasion (249, 27). James R. Gray probably had something like this in mind when he wrote, "God's initial aim is that all entities should have maximal satisfactions." (82) Gray may have confused Whitehead's metaphysical sense of "satisfaction" (definiteness and completeness) with positive hedonic feelings (69).

Whitehead's proclamation that God's aim for the world is "the evocation of intensities" is troublesome. First, in this context, he made no distinction between positive or desirable and negative or undesirable intensities of feeling. Love and compassion are desirable value-enhancing feelings, and the more intense the better. They are definitely good for us. Hatred, despair, sorrow, and physical and mental suffering and anguish are undesirable value-diminishing feelings, and the more intense the worse they are. They are bad for us, and greater intensities of them are worse. Does God aim at, and should each occasion or enduring person aim at, maximum intensity of *all* such feelings? Whitehead did not say otherwise when he identified God's purpose for the world as the evocation of intensities or feelings. He did not even consider the problem, but he should have.

Elsewhere, he was very sensitive to evil feelings and their intensities. In *Religion in the Making* he wrote, "Now evil is exhibited in physical suffering, mental suffering, and loss of the higher experience in favour of the lower experience" (95). He added, "Evil is positive and destructive; what is good is positive and creative" (96). He also said, "This is the feeling of evil in the most general sense, namely physical pain or mental evil, such as sorrow, horror, dislike" (*AI* 256).

The trouble is, *both good and evil feelings can be intense,* definite, and complete within actual occasions and enduring actual entities like us. As traditionally conceived, even the Devils in Hell aim at the evocation of maximum intensities of feeling! So did the Inquisitors, and so do sadists and today's practitioners of "enhanced interrogation techniques." Whitehead wrote occasionally about aversions, sorrows, pains, horrors, and suffering, but surely he did not have these feelings in mind when he made this unguarded statement about God's purpose in creation. The difference between positive "good for" and negative "not good for" intensities of feeling really matters!

Whitehead was also much too selective in emphasizing only feelings. Ordinarily, we distinguish feeling from thinking and acting. We consider emotions, moods, attitudes, appetites, aims, purposes, desires, pleasures, and pains to be feelings. Hartman so understood "feelings," and some of Whitehead's remarks should be so construed. At other times he seems to equate feeling with experiencing itself, but such a broad understanding of "feeling" does not help very much. It is not experiences but experiencers that have intrinsic worth. We definitely would not want all experiences to be intensified. Some experiences, aims, purposes, emotions, desires, moods, attitudes, pains, and feelings are just too horrible and undesirable.

Positive feelings, desires, appetites, emotions, moods, attitudes, affections, purposes, interests, approvals, moods, enjoyments, attitudes, etc., are abundant-life-making properties. Without feelings we would have no values at all; we would not care about anything, though we might still be able to work on a cognitive level with the abstract Form of the Good. Sentience, the capacity to have both sensory and affective feelings, is often thought to be a defining characteristic of intrinsically good creatures like us and the animals. Non-human animals (rational by degrees) as well as human animals (also rational by degrees) experience many kinds or qualities of feelings, pleasures, and pains, so feeling properties are not distinctively human. Many non-human living subjects have conscious evaluative feelings, so they also have intrinsic worth. Animals value self and others, but mere things and mere thoughts do not. Some feelings (e.g., hatred, malice, and revenge) are among our moral-bad-making properties. Having feelings partly accounts for our intrinsic goodness and well-being and partly for our inherent evil. Feelings are integral to intrinsic moral goodness, particularly feelings of profound love, empathy, compassion, delight in goodness, and aesthetic and creative concentration. Moral virtues involve habits or dispositions to feel, think, and act in pro-social ways.

Even if we limit God's purpose for the world to producing *positive* feelings, we still need to know what kind of value positive feelings have, and if anything else has positive value. Did Whitehead consider feelings to be intrinsically good, extrinsically good, systemically good, good for us, good for themselves, or what? Only concrete unique valuing actual entities, not abstractions, systemic goods, or eternal objects are intrinsically good. Positive feelings are good for us, but not good to or for themselves, for they are not selves. Valuing only feelings overlooks extrinsic and systemic goodness—embodiment, acting, thinking, knowing. Some highly "romantic" or "sentimental" human beings try to be God-like by intensifying positive feelings, nothing more. These "spiritual gluttons" aim exclusively at intense emotions, desires, pleasures, or ecstasies; but they are practically inept and mentally dim! Agreeable feelings can be greatly overvalued, to the neglect of practical (doing) and conceptual (thinking and knowing) values.

Some people really are very much like this. We might call them "emotionalists," "romanticists," or "love slobs." They have a value astigmatism; they are well developed in emotions and other feelings, but they are poorly developed practically (extrinsically) and conceptually (systemically). Whitehead probably did not mean to be so one-sided when he emphasizing feelings, but he did not make it clear that more than feelings must be intensified if we are to live abundant and worthwhile human lives. According to John Goheen, Whitehead conceived "of value itself as identical with feeling" (452). But surely God values more than and wants more for and from us than intense feelings!

To his credit, Whitehead was not always so narrowly focused in identifying "aims." "Morality," he wrote, "is always the aim at that union of harmony, intensity, and vividness which involves the perfection of importance for that occasion" (*MT* 14). This *aesthetic* formulation of aims suffers from indefiniteness and narrowness. Its three value properties—harmony, intensity, and vividness—still leave us wondering, what kind(s) of harmony, intensity, and vividness? If limited to harmonious, intense, and vivid feelings, we have made little progress. Something more than feelings alone should be harmonized, intensified, and vividified. Why not a harmony, intensity, vividness, and balance of systemic, extrinsic, and intrinsic values—all three? All are necessary for our self-realization and well-being.

We must ask also, "Harmony, intensity, and vividness *for whom?*" Whitehead's answer was very unsatisfactory: "for that occasion," and "in an occasion," he said. Are morality and aesthetics really so narrowly focused that they aim only for goodness that endures for only a fraction of a second—"that occasion"? Surely not! Why not say that morality and God aim at optimum goodness of all kinds over the long run for all enduring souls? Whitehead clearly recognized the importance of both endurance and aims toward the future. "Subjective aim," he wrote, "whereby there is origination of conceptual feeling, is at intensity of feeling . . . in the immediate subject, and . . . in the relevant future." He acknowledged that "morality hinges on the determination of relevance in the future" (*PR* 27). John Cobb clearly oriented morality toward the future.

> First, we are called to realize value in each moment. Second, we are called to determine the present in such a way that it will contribute value to the future. Whitehead thinks of the former aspect of the goal as primarily aesthetic, the latter as moral. But the moral aim for future occasions is primarily at their realization of aesthetic value in the future. (Cobb, Epperly, Nancarrow 110)

This chapter of this book argues that beauty and other related aesthetic values are not axiologically fundamental. They are not intrinsically good. They are only good for us.

GOD'S PURPOSE AS THE CREATION OF BEAUTY

Whitehead also said, "The real world is good when it is beautiful" (*AI* 264), and "The teleology of the Universe is directed to the production of

Beauty" (265). Henning thinks that creating beauty is the purpose of the universe (6, 98-100), and so do Cobb (1965, 180) and Griffin (2000, 293, 300). The trouble is, as they stand, these affirmations do not explicitly recognize or appreciate the fact that conscious individuals, God included, are experiencing and being enriched by such beauty, and that the real value of all beauty is for them. Enduring, conscious, unique, valuing individuals are irrelevant to these aesthetic pronouncements as they stand. Whitehead and other process thinkers may *presuppose* that the real world is beautiful *for individuals,* but it would be helpful for them to say so emphatically and consistently. Then it would be much harder for them to reduce ethics to aesthetics.

Beauty is only one among many secondary "good for" aspects of what benefits unique souls, and of the world's overall goodness. It would be much more accurate to say that the real world is good when it contains unique, intrinsically valuable, enduring centers or subjects of awareness, consciousness, experience, understanding, feeling, and activity whose well-being is constantly being enriched by concretely ingressed eternal objects such as beauty, pleasure, thought, reason, truth, knowledge, free choices, creativity, freedom, novelty, adventure, self-awareness, love for self, concern for others, regard for the whole of reality, love and compassion for others, positive emotions, desires, and affections, moral activities, virtues, growth, self-realization, spirituality, God-awareness, etc. Our well-being is also being enriched constantly, not just by instantiated universals, but by concrete individuals—God, people, animals, living things, wild things—and their friendship, companionship, and presence. Beauty is only one among the universals that enrich our souls and our well-being. Even more significantly, individual persons, families, friends, neighbors, animals, and beyond both enrich our lives and are ends in themselves. Ethics is more fundamental than aesthetics.

The process God should be reconceived as primarily an ethicist, not an aesthete. For ethics, unique, concrete, conscious, enduring, valuing self and other significant, individual subjects as ends in themselves are axiologically basic; for aesthetics, beauty is the ultimate axiological value.

GOD'S PURPOSE AS CREATING INTRINSICALLY VALUABLE ACTUAL ENTITIES

Consider now an alternative proposal for God's purpose for the universe, one compatible with Whitehead's "The purpose of God is the attainment of value in the temporal world" (*RM* 100). God's purpose for this and every world is to create intrinsically valuable unique subjects of value and valuation. Instead of saying that God's purpose is to create intensities of feeling or beauty, Whitehead should have said that God's purpose for the world is to create, "each in its due season," as he once remarked (*AI* 277), all compossible degrees and kinds of unique, intrinsically valuable, enduring, experiencing, self and other valuing, and partly self-creative and self-actualizing psychophysical subjects who are constantly being enriched in an incredible variety of positive ways by "good for" properties like beauty, prosperity, creativity, adventure, freedom, responsibility, pleasure, intense *positive* feelings and affections, love, concern, and compassion for others, knowledge, truth, behavioral guidelines, moral goodness or virtue, fruitful and enjoyable activities, etc.—even at the risk of conflict and evil. Whitehead stressed that "the teleology of the Universe" aims at "variety" as well as "intensity" (201). He advocated "rating types of order in relative importance according to their success in magnifying the individualities" (290), but the significance of this depends on what he meant by "individualities," and on what exactly is to be magnified. Instead of emphasizing God's "particular providence for particular occasions" (*PR* 532), Whitehead should have emphasized God's particular providence for an inconceivable-to-us diversity of unique, enduring, valuing, actual entities.

Creating all logically possible concrete unique self-and-other valuing actualities is a task for Infinity. This would require many worlds in infinite supertime, well beyond the limits of our 13.7 billion years old universe. It would also require infinite superspace containing an "ensemble" of universes existing well beyond, endlessly beyond, the finite region of our own spacetime system, and infinitely before its paltry 13.7 billion years. In our finitude, we cannot fathom such infinite creativity or love. God's creativity can never use up infinity. When Whitehead postulated "cosmic epochs" other than our own, he used the *spatial* word *"beyond"* more than once to describe them (*PR* 95, 288). He never said *"before,"* but that is the way that most process metaphysicians interpret other cosmic epochs. "Beyond" does not require temporal antecedents and allows that some universes might be created out of nothing, but most process metaphysicians assume that our universe was created from the residual "big crunch" chaos of some temporally antecedent universe located in an oscillating series of universes extending all the way back to infinity.

Process thinkers have generally rejected the view that God created our universe out of nothing at some point in the finite past. They think that a loving God will always have a world to love, and that *ex nihilo* creation ascribes too much power to God. Yet, a viable theology must find the mean between giving God too much power and not enough power. Just how much is enough, and for what purposes, are complicated issues that are always resolved in terms of what we (or theologians) value. We need to become our own theologians.

There are many difficulties with the standard process appeal to antecedent oscillating universes, each of which ended in the lingering chaos of a big crunch, and one of which created our own universe, with God's persuasion. That longer story has been told elsewhere (Edwards 2001, Ch. 4). In brief, to make this work, an unverifiable to us infinite series of such universes in supertime must be presupposed, or else the first universe in the series would have been created *ex nihilo*. More importantly, our universe definitely does not fit into such a series because, as discovered in 1998, it is both expanding and *its rate of expansion is increasing* (71-72, 106-107). This means that it will never crunch, as did its infinitely many supposed antecedents, and it will thus have no successors. It just does not fit the "infinite series" pattern assumed by most process theologians. It may not have been, but if it was created from the Big Bang of a singularity, singularities are empirical nothingness, not residual chaos (92-94). As most process theologians see it, what exactly is the difference between the lingering chaos of an antecedent universe from which our universe was made and the nothingness of traditional *ex nihilo* theology? What remains of the previous universe in this chaos? This residual chaos brought forward must have retained some minimal causation or energy (Enough to make another universe?) as well as some spatial (How big? How compact?), temporal (Discrete actual occasions?), and lawful (increasing entropy—from chaos?) properties, but absolutely none of this remains in singularities.

Modern astrophysists have no difficulty conceiving of a time before our time or a space beyond our space—an infinitely old superspacetime that houses "multiple universes." They do not seem to realize that they have stepped into that mysterious realm of "unverifiable metaphysics" where philosophers and theologians dwell. Doing theology self-consciously for a moment, each universe in superspacetime could be created *ex nihilo* by God without violating the process principle that a loving God "always" has some world to love (Edwards 2000, 77-96; 2001, 257-74). This does *not* mean, however, that a loving God would necessarily create *all logically possible* universes, for some might be too horrible for God's love to bear. To conceive of what we really cannot imagine, an infinitely creative God would produce only all logically possible *good* universes within infinite superspace and supertime. Such universes would be populated by intrinsically valuable individuals capable of enjoying beauty, feeling profoundly, and living ethically.

IS THE DISPUTE MERELY VERBAL?

If the controversy over whether aesthetics or ethics is most basic in process thought is anything more than a purely verbal quibble, there must be a real difference between them. *For ethics, unique conscious subjects are axiologically fundamental; for aesthetics, beauty is fundamental.* Of course, this whole dispute may be only a purely verbal quibble, at least in part. Ethics must first judge what is "important" and then aim at its actualization or maximization, but what if, by definition, all judgments of importance are automatically classified as "aesthetic"?

Consider "importance" in the sense of "intrinsically good." One way to turn the quibble over aesthetics versus ethics into a purely verbal dispute would be to arbitrarily classify or define everything intrinsically good or important as an "aesthetic" value. Hartshorne pursed this strategy when he wrote, "Since the intrinsic value of experiences is by definition aesthetic value, and since goodness is the disinterested will to enhance the value of future experience, ethics presupposes aesthetics" (1970, 308).

One difficulty is that Hartshorne here identifies *experiences* as such, not *experiencing individuals,* as intrinsically valuable. That leaves experiencing individuals with the worth of useful buckets for holding the good stuff, but otherwise worthless. But suppose he had said something like, "Since the intrinsic value of experiencing individuals is by definition aesthetic value . . . ethics presupposes aesthetics." The quibble over ethics versus aesthetics would indeed be merely verbal if any candidate for "intrinsically good" is defined as "aesthetic," and if "ethics" is never allowed to make such judgments.

Hartshorne did treat all intrinsic value as aesthetic value when he wrote, "The study that concerns itself with value in its universal character is esthetics, taken in the broadest sense. Esthetic value is immediate value, and this all experience must present, and to this all mediate value must lead" (1953, 44). One problem here is that axiology, not aesthetics, is what concerns itself with value in its universal character. The proper subdivisions of axiology are ethics, aesthetics, logic, religion, and all disciplines that make or presuppose norms. Whitehead himself made such distinctions (*MT* 11, 26). Turning all intrinsic value into aesthetic value by definition merely begs the question and offers an unsuccessful verbal solution to current problems.

A substantive disagreement is present here. This chapter brings it into focus with a much less contrived classification of unique experiencing individuals as intrinsic ethical values, and beauty, its degrees, and its variations as aesthetic values. This substantive disagreement is here resolved in favor of the priority of unique experiencing individuals, and this makes ethics more fundamental than aesthetics.

If beauty, positive intensities, pleasures etc., have only "good for" value but not intrinsic worth, the claim that God's purpose or aim for the world is to create beauty is equivalent to saying that God aims fundamentally at producing something that has no intrinsic worth. Beauty, even for or as enjoyed by God, is just one "good for" property among all the others, even if collectively, all diverse intrinsically valuable individuals and their good-making properties were all so arranged as to be perfectly harmonious and beautiful. (They aren't; the problem of evil stands in the way inexorably.)

Claiming that beauty is the only or the primary good is like insisting, as hedonists do, that pleasure is the only or the most primary good. Both beauty and pleasure are good for us, but so are many, many other things. Unique, enduring, experiencing, self-realizing, self-valuing, and other-valuing conscious individuals, not beauty, and not pleasure, are metaphysically and morally basic. The intrinsic value of unique individuals is the central value of ethics, not of aesthetics.

The proper aims of ethics or morality will be more carefully considered in later chapters. For now, consider Hartshorne's second but closely related way of distinguishing ethics from aesthetics, as expressed in two closely related quotes.

> What basically is value? It cannot be ethical value that is basic; for ethics is concerned with consequences or with justice to others; and the goodness or badness of these consequences, or the good and bad that is to be justly distributed, must be measured by a criterion other than the ethical. (1953, 44)

> Ethical value, goodness, is not the value of experiences themselves, but rather the instrumental value of acting so as to increase the intrinsic value of future experiences, particularly those of others than oneself. (1970, 308)

Here Hartshorne again attempts another purely verbal solution to our problem. He *defines ethics* purely extrinsically as "the instrumental value of acting." Thereby he again arbitrarily excludes all judgments of intrinsic good and evil from the domain of ethics. Other than making it so by arbitrary definition, I see no good reason for excluding judgments of intrinsic goodness from ethics, and I believe that most moral philosophers would agree. Recall G.E. Moore's three questions of *ethics,* slightly paraphrased: What does "good" mean? What things are good? and What ought I to do? A more refined account of the nature of ethics will be developed in later chapters, but classifying judgments of intrinsic worth as "ethical" should be allowed. If allowed, ethics is more fundamental than aesthetics.

4.

"GOOD," AND WHAT AND HOW WE VALUE

Whitehead never defined "good" or "importance" as such, though he identified "intrinsically good" with "self-significance" or "self-enjoyment." Robert S. Hartman's formal axiology offers a general axiological definition of "good" that significantly supplements Whitehead. Formal axiology can contribute substance, clarity, and systematic orderliness to process philosophy's answers to G.E. Moore's first two questions of ethics: "What does 'good' mean?" and "What things are good?" Hartman gave very plausible answers to these two questions. An axiological process understanding of intrinsic goodness was developed in the preceding chapter. "What things are good?" Unique individual persons and other unique conscious self- and other-valuing individuals such as God, the animals, and beyond. This new chapter addresses Moore's first question of ethics: "What is the meaning of 'good'?" Then, other kinds of goodness are identified.

DEFINING "GOOD"

So, what does "good" mean? How should we define this word or concept? Process thinkers answer G.E. Moore's second question, but they greatly neglect his first. Today, "What does 'good' mean?" would be classified as a "meta-ethical" rather than as an "ethical" question. Process thinkers emphasize many *good things*—somewhat unsystematically, I should add: truth, reason, knowledge, intense feeling, harmony, beauty, unity in variety, works of art, richness of experience, creativity, novelty, zest, freedom, adventure, peace, enjoyment, self-enjoyment, love, compassion, etc. But they offer no analysis of the meaning of "good," especially not one that includes and applies to all good things, whether intrinsic or not. They may think this unimportant, or they may simply equate good things with the meaning of "good," thus committing Moore's infamous "naturalistic fallacy." I am not the first to notice process thought's inadequacies in value theory, especially in understanding "The Good." Paul Arthur Schilpp noticed this as early as 1941 (563-618, especially 592ff), but this problems still persist. To get a sense for this, look for "good" in the indexes of the many books on process ethics and theology published in the last twenty five years. You will not find it in most, and when you do, the references are always to good things, not to the meaning of "good" itself. Even with "Good" in the title, there is no index entry for "good" in Herman E. Daly and John B. Cobb, Jr., *For the Common Good*.

Hartman's formal axiology can do better. The "axiom" of his formal axiology is his definition of "good:" "Good is concept (or standard) fulfillment." This is a real and workable formal definition. G.E. Moore insisted that the concept is indefinable; but this is not a "naturalistic" definition that identifies "good" with "good things" such as those mentioned in the preceding paragraph. Robert S. Hartman, the creator of formal axiology, spent many years searching for and sifting through innumerable definitions and uses of "good" in order to discover its common meaning (1994, 51-52). G.E. Moore, whose *Principia Ethica* was published in 1901, had more impact on ethical thinking in the 20th century than almost anyone else. With Moore, Hartman agreed that "good" is not synonymous with any natural or descriptive property like pleasure, happiness, satisfaction, desire fulfillment, interest, preference, approval, knowledge, truth, conscientiousness, and so on. Such definitions commit the "naturalistic fallacy," where answers to "What is the meaning of 'good'?" are confused with answers to "What things are good?" Moore concluded from his own philosophical investigations that "good" can not be defined at all, but Hartman disagreed. He showed successfully that this key value concept can *be defined formally, though not materially or naturalistically.* "Good" can be defined after all, the naturalistic fallacy can be avoided, and the intimate relationship between the "Form of the Good" and descriptive "good-making properties" can be made clear. "Descriptive" or "natural" is construed very broadly and not limited to "sensory." Descriptive properties are actual properties like pleasures, even if they exist only within conscious souls.

Both G.E. Moore and Whitehead wondered about how facts and values are related, but neither solved the problem. According to Whitehead, "Value refers to Fact, and Fact refers to Value" (*SP* 88), but he told us nothing about what "refers to" really means. G.E. Moore puzzled over the intimate but not identical relation between facts and values for most of his career, but he never solved the problem to his satisfaction, or anyone else's. Hartman solved the problem: Facts are the good-making properties contained within the Form of the Good. Just what this means will be explained shortly.

Whitehead's own essay on "Mathematics and the Good" did not get very far. It had very few helpful things to say about the meaning of "Good." He recognized at its beginning that the distinguished audience who came to hear Plato's lecture on "The Notion of The Good" must have been very disappointed. "The lecture was a failure, so far as concerned the elucidation of its professed topic; for the lecturer mainly devoted himself to Mathematics" (*SP* 105). After reading Whitehead's own essay, we keenly sense the same failure. He too mainly discussed mathematics and had very little to say about the good and its connection with mathematics. He made no more progress when he returned to the topic of mathematics and the good in *Modes of Thought* (76-82). His "Mathematics and the Good" did make two very abstruse but important points that are relevant to our present concerns. First, he redefined "mathematics" as "the intellectual analysis of types of pattern" (117, 120). Second, he recognized that "the Good" has something to do with patterns (117, 118).

THE FORM OF THE GOOD

The main problem is, Whitehead had nothing to say about the *kind of pattern* involved in "the Good." Hartman did. He offered a formal definition of "good" that actually captures what Plato called "the Form of the Good," the *formal pattern* common to all judgments of goodness. In common, all "X is good" judgments match the actual descriptive properties of some X with someone's ideal expectations for entities belonging to the class or concept of X. These descriptive predicates comprise someone's concept of an ideal X. The descriptive or actual properties of good Xs fulfill or match the ideal predicates contained in the normative standards being applied to them. Such properties are their "good-making properties." A good X is as it is supposed to be; it has *all* the good-making properties called for by its formal or conceptual norm, standard, or concept. A fair X has most of them, an average X has about half, a poor X has relatively few, and a bad or no-good X has almost no good-making properties at all. That is what "good" and degrees thereof mean, and that is how facts are related to values.

Whitehead recognized that "There cannot be value without antecedent standards of value" (*SMW* 178). Formal axiology's definition of "The Form of the Good" is this: "Good is concept or standard fulfillment." As Hartman himself expressed it, *"A thing is good if it fulfills the intension of its concept"* (Hartman, 1967, 103, 153). This means that if you want to know whether ANYTHING is good, you must:

A. have a standard or "concept" at your disposal, consisting of an indefinite number of ideal conceptual good-making descriptive predicates applicable to the objects being evaluated;

B. examine or otherwise learn "second hand" about the value objects to determine their actual properties;

C. match their actual properties with the ideal predicates they are supposed to have;

D. finally, judge or conclude that they are good if they have all the properties they are supposed to have, or judge them to be good by degrees (fair, average, poor, no good) if they have some but not all of them (Edwards, 2010, 2-7).

Anyone can become a better judge of value by understanding that legitimate or rationally justified judgments of "good" always involve these four steps. This "Form of the Good" works for understanding a good God, a good religion, a good politician, a morally good person, a good car, a good business, a good theory or belief, or a good anything.

Values are *meanings* in the sense that they always involve both the intensional connotations and the extensional denotations of concepts. Thus, the most valuable life is the most meaningful life, and the most meaningful life is the most valuable life.

Philosophers have sought it since the time of Plato, but for the first time in human history, Robert S. Hartman "saw" the "Form of the Good," common to all its uses. This is what the bare Form of the Good looks like:

GOOD-MAKING PREDICATES	ACTUAL PROPERTIES
1. _____	1. _____
2. _____	2. _____
3. _____	3. _____
4. _____	4. _____

5. _____   5. _____

6. _____   6. _____

We can fail to reach agreement or make mistakes in positive value judgments if we:

A. disagree about or misunderstand which good-making predicates are included in the ideal standard,

B. fail to examine, learn about, or understand adequately the actual properties of the value-object to which it is being applied,

C. mis-match a thing's actual properties with its ideal predicates, or

D. fail to draw logical conclusions.

This form can be applied to everything about which anyone makes positive value judgments, whether intrinsic, extrinsic, systemic, moral, non-moral, or whatever. A corresponding form for "bad" or "evil" consists of bad-making predicates, though this negative form is not emphasized here (Edwards 2010, 7-9) and was not developed by Hartman. The forms of "good" and "bad" are definitive or absolute in structure or theory, but particular standards that fit these forms are always subjective and context-relative in application. Disagreements or errors may occur anywhere between A. and D above, especially at point A (Hartman, 1967, 110-11). When that happens, to make further progress, such disagreements and errors must be discussed and resolved, perhaps using additional and more intricate applications of the Form of the Good. Sometimes we just have to agree to disagree. Very often, we will reach agreement if we understand and make use of the Form of the Good. Hartman's Form of the Good really works! Process philosophers and theologians with axiological concerns would do well to take advantage of it.

Our ideal standards may vary, and they may come from many sources—our linguistic and cultural traditions, influential others, our moral intuitions, or our own personal preferences and creative choices. As Hartman pointed out, this formal definition of good "is objective. It is valid for every rational being whatever . . . But its application is subjective." (1967, 110) This means that we can disagree about which standards to accept and apply. Norms may vary from person to person, culture to culture, or situation to situation, but the Form of the Good is always the same: Good things actually exemplify the good-making properties of the concepts (the ideal sets of good-making predicates) that we apply to them.

Expressed more simply, good things measure up to their ideals. Their actual properties match their ideal predicates. Whitehead defined *"conceptual experience"* as "the entertainment of possibilities for ideal realization in abstraction from any sheer physical realization. The most obvious example of conceptual experience is the entertainment of alternatives" (*MT* 166-67). Alternative possibilities must be both entertained and assessed or ranked. Supposedly, actual occasions can do this in less than a tenth of a second! Real people take longer.

Consider a realistic process example. A typical process understanding of "a good human life" might be something like this. People have good lives to the extent that their lives actualize and include such good-making descriptive properties as truth, reason, knowledge, intense feeling, harmony, beauty, unity in variety, art, richness of experience, imagination, creativity, novelty, freedom, adventure, zest, peace, enjoyment, self-enjoyment, love, compassion, significant others, and so on. These abstract good-life-making universals can be instantiated or ingressed by degrees within unique concrete persons, animals, etc. A fulfilled life self-actualizes these ideal properties or eternal objects. Most of these good-making properties are not distinctively human, so animals as well as people may live good lives, fair lives, average lives, poor lives, or no-good lives, depending on (a) which ideal aims are supplied by God, reflection, nature, culture, preference, or choice, and (b) the degree to which ideal good-making properties are actualized. Living a good life obviously takes time, and self-realization is an ongoing process.

Moral goodness will be covered in the next chapter, but there are many kinds of goodness in addition to intrinsic and moral goodness. Many very good things are neither intrinsic nor moral goods, for example: good food, good workers, good products, good tools, good clothes, good cars, a good education, good theories, good societies, etc. As Whitehead recognized, "Morals constitute only one aspect of the good, an aspect often overstressed" (*MT* 76). Importance, Whitehead's "generic notion" for axiological goodness, has "innumerable species" such as morality, logic, religion, art, beauty, etc. (*MT* 11, 26). Axiology, the most general theory of value, deals with every kind of goodness or importance. Formal Axiology differs from other approaches in concentrating first and foremost on the general patterns or forms involved in all value experiences, feelings, judgments, preferences, choices, and applications. If, as Whitehead said, mathematics deals with patterns, then axiology successfully applies mathematics to all instances of goodness! Hartman himself went even further than this. He developed a formal calculus of value by applying transfinite math to the three dimensions of goodness explained later, but I see too many problems with the way he did it (Edwards, 2010, 67-82).

Ethically, people ought to be valued intrinsically as ends in themselves, but we often value people in many other ways, and it is not always immoral so to do. It is morally wrong to treat people as *mere means*, as Kant said, but not wrong to value and treat them as *means* as long as their intrinsic worth is respected in thoughts, attitudes, and actions. Managers, department heads, or employers assess and rank the workplace usefulness of employees annually or periodically. When this happens, nothing immoral is going on—as long as the employer also respects the employee intrinsically and thinks, feels, and acts accordingly by providing fair wages, benefits, safe and friendly working conditions, and so on. Understanding and using the Form of the Good can greatly facilitate this process. What exactly does the employer expect? Does the employee have it? If not, does the employee need more training, discipline, effort, or what?

Consider a case that acceptably applies an extrinsic "usefulness" standard to an intrinsically valuable person employed as a college teacher. If Prof. X is an extrinsically good or useful college teacher, he must not only actually exemplify the defining predicates of "college teacher," but he (or she) must also exemplify the additional ideal expositional "good-making" predicates of the college teacher social role. He must:

(Definitional predicates)

1. actually be a teacher,

2. be employed to teach by a college,

(Additional expositional extrinsic good-making predicates)

3. know well his subject matter,

4. engage in research and publication in his areas of teaching and specialization,

5. keep up with the latest developments in his areas of teaching and specialization,

6. be effective in communicating with students,

7. be fair and unprejudiced in grading students' papers and other course work,

8. make himself readily available to students, e.g. by keeping regular office hours,

9. encourage his students who do well,

10. give extra help and attention to students who need it, etc.

Taking adequate account of the intrinsic goodness of Prof. X (or anyone) involves the five intrinsic good-making properties discussed in Chapter Two. Taking account of anyone's *moral* goodness will be discussed in Chapter Five. But taking account of the *professional extrinsic goodness* of college teachers involves something like the above ideal set of good-making descriptive predicates. There are many kinds of goodness, but the Form of the Good fits them all.

This list of the good-making predicates of college teachers could be extended almost indefinitely, as the "etc." indicates. Other professional norms or expectations might apply, but criteria like these are widely used to determine if any given college teacher is extrinsically good, useful, or "professional." This is what a good college teacher is supposed to be like. Expectations are built into our basic understanding of all of our social roles. The norms (good-making predicates) in the above list largely constitute our concept of "good college teacher." All of our social concepts are normative. None are ever "purely descriptive."

Assuming that this list is sufficient, then if Prof. X exemplifies all ten of these good-making predicates, he (or she) is indeed a good college teacher. To be classified as a college teacher at all, he must fulfill the first two defining criteria. The remaining expositional good-making predicates may be fulfilled by degrees, so Prof. X would be a good college teacher if he completely fulfills the ten-point standard. If he fulfills the ten criteria only partly or by degrees he would be only fair, average, poor, or close to worthless as a college teacher. Good is *complete* standard or concept fulfillment.

DEFINING "BETTER," "BEST," AND "OUGHT"

Beginning with Whitehead, process thinkers have offered many variations on the theme of God's aims or purposes for the world and for human beings. Another variation involves the concept of "best." In *The Call of the Spirit: Process Spirituality in a Relational World* by John B. Cobb, Jr., Bruce G. Epperly, and Paul S. Nancarrow, the authors say that God aims at, and we should aim at, what is best. As Cobb put it, "God calls us to be and to do what is best" (24, 110; compare Epperly, 124), but no account of the meaning of "best" is given. Process thinkers neglect the task of defining both "good" and "best." We do not know how these authors define "best"?

Formal axiology offers plausible and useful formal definitions of "good," "better," and "best." We now understand that "good" things exemplify the good-making descriptive or actual properties contained in the norms or standards applied to them. "Better" and "best" also involve sets of good-making properties. If X and Y belong to the same class of comparison, X is better than Y if X has more relevant good-making properties than Y. X is the best of the lot if it exemplifies more good-making properties than all the others in its class of comparison (Edwards 2010, 20-22).

The Form of the Good can be used to *make comparative judgments* and ascertain who or what is best. If two established college teachers, Prof. X and Prof. Y, are candidates for a new position, Prof. X is the best candidate if he has nine out of ten of the identified good-making properties, and Prof. Y has only seven. Though not perfectly good, Prof. X is the best of the lot if only two teachers are being compared. Some Super X would be absolutely best or "Supreme," like God, if this Super X exemplifies all consistently combinable perfect-making properties, including the property of creating free and co-creative creatures, and that of constant and creative self-surpassing. Formal axiology's paraphrase of St. Anselm is: God is that being than whom none richer in perfect-making properties can be conceived.

Hartman defined "better" in terms of "richness." "Better" means "Richer in properties," he wrote (1967, 114). Adding "good-making" to his definition to get "richer in good-making properties" improves his definition because "worse" and "worst" also involve richness in properties—bad-making ones. Hartman seldom discussed bad-making properties and usually treated bad as nothing more than privation of good-making properties. Axiologically, "best" means "richest in good-making properties," and "worst" means "richest in bad-making properties" (1957, 208).

I wholeheartedly agree with Cobb that "God calls us to be and to do what is best." Process thinkers are definitely on the right track here, but this should be construed to mean that God calls us to live lives that are as rich as we can make them in good-making properties of all kinds, that is, in all value dimensions, not just in feelings alone, thoughts alone, deeds alone, or beauty alone. Our day-to-day choices are often between options that are richer or poorer in goodness, and we should always select the richest and best, recognizing that goodness is multi-dimensional.

Cobb and Nancarrow emphasized richness of *experience,* though they only sketchily explain and illustrate this. Cobb wrote, "God calls each human occasion of experience to actualize the richest possibility in the new moment" (31), and Nancarrow suggested, "God's purpose in the world is the evocation of ever-richer forms of experience" (53, 55, 90, 131, 135). But what does this "richness" involve? Richness of what? And for whom? Richness cannot credibly be reduced to intense positive feelings, to aesthetic abstractions, or to any one value dimension—the intrinsic alone, the extrinsic alone, the systemic alone, (or the aesthetic alone). A human life that exemplifies maximal richness in all three value dimensions is better (richer in good-making properties) than a life that is almost exclusively intrinsic, or extrinsic, or systemic. A truly abundant human life requires optimal personal development in all three dimensions of goodness. Otherwise, a life even richer in good-making properties is conceivable. People who do not develop themselves in all three value dimensions are axiologically challenged and have serious "problems in living," as psychologists would say. We aspire to live as abundantly as we possibly can.

Finally, formal axiology offers a plausible and workable definition of "ought." "X ought to be done" means "X is the best thing to do, so do it" (Edwards 2010, 134-35). This defines "ought" teleologically and captures its conventional imperative force. "Ought" aims at promoting goodness, or at the best of the lot when making comparisons. Ought judgments commend as well as connote. "Should" usually means "ought." Because it makes a place for "ought" judgments, process ethics is sometimes called "deontological." However, its "ought" is defined teleologically. It requires acting to achieve the greatest possible goodness for everyone's sake, not ought or duty for its own sake.

THREE DIMENSIONS OF GOODNESS: SYSTEMIC, EXTRINSIC, AND INTRINSIC

We now understand the meaning of "good" and will return to G.E. Moore's second questions of ethics, "What things are good?" There is no simple answer to this question because there are many different kinds of goodness. As Moore understood his own question, it was probably about intrinsic goodness, but formal axiology recognizes at least three different dimensions or kinds of goodness. The door is open for even more kinds if anyone can discover and differentiate them. Different value-objects or "things that are good" will fall into any one of three distinct value dimensions. All three involve concept or standard fulfillment, the Form of the

Good. The three are: *systemic, extrinsic, and intrinsic*. All of them can be measured or compared rationally or conceptually with respect to their degree of goodness (Edwards 2010, 27-39), so they fall into a rationally ordered *hierarchy of value,* as explained shortly.

Systemic goods are desirable mental or conceptual values. Primary examples are: concepts, ideas, constructs, words, propositions, beliefs, doctrines, philosophical, theological, and scientific systems, laws, rules, principles, mathematical and logical forms, ritual patterns, and formalities of every description.

Extrinsic goods are means to ends beyond themselves. They include pragmatically valuable or useful actions, objects, processes, and activities located in public space-time and known through ordinary sensory perception. Examples are: beneficial human behaviors, natural resources, tools, artifacts, flowing water, drinkable water, nutritious foods, shelters, clothing, etc. For short, we will call such aggregates "mere things" since macroscopically, except for some foods, they are inanimate and lack evaluative consciousness. Hartman limited extrinsic goodness itself to useful external sensory objects, processes, and actions, but he recognized that other goods (e.g., people or ideas) can be valued for their usefulness, as if they were extrinsic goods.

Intrinsic goods are ends in themselves, desirable for their own sakes, valuable in, to, and for themselves. Primary examples are individual persons and other unique, enduring, conscious, embodied, valuing souls like God and the animals. They have in common the five defining properties of "intrinsically good" developed in Chapter Two. Intrinsically valuable entities are not conceptual abstractions or mindless physical objects and processes. They are unique conscious subjects of experience, thought, feeling, action, and valuation in all of their definiteness and concreteness.

Without using our technical vocabulary for it, Whitehead himself came very close to identifying these three dimensions of goodness, and to ranking them and recognizing the inadequacies of systemic and extrinsic values alone when he wrote,

> There is something between the gross specialized values of the mere practical man, and the thin specialized values of the mere scholar. Both types have missed something; and if you add together the two sets of values, you do not obtain the missing elements. What is wanted is an appreciation of the infinite variety of vivid values achieved by an organism in its proper environment. (*SMW* 199)

The lives and experiences of intrinsically good actualities may be enriched in many different vivid values that are internal or psychological intrinsic-value-enriching universals (eternal objects), for example, positive feelings, moral and spiritual growth, and the other inner "good for" properties like those discussed in Chapter Three. Not just universals but other individuals also can and do enrich our lives. For Whitehead it was important that individuals can be present to and within other individuals (*SMW* 174-75, *PR* 5), but he had in mind only the presence of *fleeting* actual occasions within one another. Morally and spiritually, we are concerned about how *enduring* souls can be present within one another. We are indeed relational realities and members of one another metaphysically and axiologically. Intrinsic identification with others is a moral and spiritual way that other-person presence within self or soul is possible. External extrinsic values and internal systemic values can also enrich the lives and experiences of intrinsically valuable persons and animals.

Answers to "What things are good intrinsically?" are highly controversial. Philosophers have debated and disagreed about this for more than two millennia. G.E. Moore's answer was: consciousness of "the pleasures of human intercourse and the enjoyment of beautiful objects" (188). To this we should at least add "individuated." That unique conscious and self-significant actualities are intrinsically good is highly controversial. Both process and axiological thinkers accept this answer, but not everyone does. Most philosophers claim that repeatable universals or eternal objects, not unique individuals, are intrinsically good. Hedonists say that only pleasure (or hedonic happiness) is intrinsically good. Other philosophers support desire-fulfillment, or truth, or knowledge, or moral conscientiousness, or beauty, or some other eternal object, as intrinsic goods. By contrast, axiological process ethics affirms that unique individuals are intrinsically good.

MOORE'S PRINCIPLE OF ISOLATION

The only *method* philosophers have ever discovered for determining which entities are intrinsically good is the "Principle of Isolation," as named and described by G.E. Moore (91-96, 187-89). The method itself is ancient and was used by Plato and Aristotle. This method involves isolating the item being considered from all else with which it is normally associated, then determining intuitively whether we desire it in itself or for its own sake when so isolated. We may discover that we value it only for its mental or conceptual worth, or only as a means to an end beyond itself, or as good for something else besides itself. After carefully applying Moore's method of isolation, if we find intuitively that something all by itself is desirable as an end in itself or for its own sake, we can reasonably proclaim it to be intrinsically good. Procedurally, our five defining properties of intrinsically good things emerge from discovering what is common to entities first judged to be good using the method of isolation.

Discerning *what things* are intrinsically valuable using Moore's "method of isolation" is relatively straightforward when dealing with fairly simple and self-contained candidates like pleasures, cars, cash, and truths, but applying it to complex and inherently relational entities like individual persons is much more complicated. When considering realities that largely consist of their internal relations with other people and the universe, how can we isolate them in thought, experience, and imagination from everything else with which they are normally associated? As Brian Henning correctly indicates, "In a processive cosmos, individuality does not imply independence," and "Hence, an individual is what it is because it is internally and essentially related to other achieved values" (60).

Still, it makes some sense to consider what unique individual persons are "in themselves," even if such "selves" are inherently social and relational. Even after we acknowledge the vastness and relatedness of every distinctive person's total set of social affections, dispositions, derivations, capabilities, personal projects, influences, experiences, preferences, choices, actions, etc., we can still distinguish and thereby "isolate" enduring entities that are unique, conscious, individuated, and self or other valuing, from those that are not, for instance, mindless aggregates or material things, and soul-dependent pleasures, truth, beauty, creativity, etc. Whitehead did not doubt that it makes sense to consider "the value of an individual for itself" as well as "the value of the diverse individuals of the world for each other," and "the value of the objective world" (*RM* 59). If intuitively we find that only unique conscious individuals who value themselves and others are ends in themselves and valuable for their own sakes, we have successfully applied the method of isolation.

Commonly advanced as candidates for "intrinsically good" are universals like sustained pleasure (hedonic happiness), desire fulfillment, truth, knowledge, conscientiousness, etc. After reflecting for almost a lifetime on them and trying out a few for size, my own carefully considered and rationally refined judgment is that these are not intrinsically good. They have some other kind of goodness. They exist only within us and are very good for us, but they are not good in, to, or for themselves.

Whitehead affirmed, "In philosophical writings proof should be at a minimum. The whole effort should be to display the self-evidence of basic truths, concerning the nature of things and their connection" (*MT* 48). Using the method of isolation, here is an easy way to *see intuitively* that pleasure, truth, beauty, etc. are not to be valued for their own sake. Carefully applying this method to them means separating them from all else with which they are normally associated, including individual conscious actualities like ourselves. Considered rigorously only "in themselves" or "in isolation," such candidates for "intrinsically good" cannot even exist, much less have positive value. They mean nothing to themselves; they do not value themselves or anything else. They exist only in us or in other conscious or experiencing individuals. They are thus good only in, to, and for us but not in, to, or for themselves. Only unique, conscious or experiencing, enduring, self-significant actualities are ends in themselves or intrinsic goods. On this insight was based the definition of "intrinsic good" offered earlier. Other very desirable internal goods are only intrinsic value enrichers or enhancers. They are good for intrinsically valuable individuals, people, animals, souls.

As noted earlier, Immanuel Kant (52-53) got the words right when he said that we should always treat persons as ends in themselves [intrinsic goods], and never merely as means [extrinsic goods]. Just what Kant meant by this is another story, previously told. Despite Kant, Descartes, and many other "speciesists," this ethical norm should be applied far beyond our own human kind. That would be best, so do it!

Process thinkers give diverse and sometimes fuzzy answers to "What things are good?" because they are not familiar with and do not keep track of the three dimensions of goodness. Their answers are diverse, selective, unsystematic, and often quite unclear with respect to exactly what kind of goodness their values have, that is, where their values belong within the three value dimensions. A review of the literature finds process thinkers sponsoring the goodness of such things as truth, reason, knowledge, intense feeling, harmony, beauty, unity in variety, art, richness of experience, creativity, novelty, imagination, freedom, adventure, peace, enjoyment, self-enjoyment, love, compassion, etc. Implicitly if not explicitly, Whitehead affirmed the goodness of all of these in various sections of *Adventures of Ideas* and elsewhere, but exactly what kind of goodness do they have—systemic, extrinsic, or intrinsic? No process ethicist so far has offered a comprehensive value theory that differentiates these three dimensions of goodness and pulls them all together into a systematic axiological ordered hierarchy of values. Hartmanian axiology can do better.

THE HIERARCHY OF VALUES

Whitehead recognized that "values differ in importance" (*SMW* 104). He emphasized "the grading of value" (*RM* 60) and recognized "grades of importance and types of importance" (*MT* 7). He commended rating an individual "on the double basis, partly on the intrinsic strength and reality of its own experience, and partly on its influence in the promotion of a high-grade type of order" (*AI* 292, *SMW* 104-05). He usually had natural distinctions between human beings, animals, vegetables, cells, and atoms in mind when he discussed ratings (*MT* 27-28, 156-58, 168; *PR* 177-78). He also recognized endless "grades of aesthetic beauty, which constitute the ideals of different schools and periods of art" (*SP* 95), presumably based on kinds or degrees of beauty or harmony. Regrettably, Whitehead told us very little about what grading values involves or how to do it. Formal axiology offers guidelines for ranking degrees and kinds of goodness, and these can illuminate more clearly not only the natural and aesthetic distinctions that Whitehead had in mind but also many other significant value differences and combinations.

According to formal axiology, intrinsically good things have more good-making properties than extrinsically good things, which in turn have more good-making properties than systemically good things. This "more" can be qualitative as well as quantitative. Qualitative differences (e.g., "good for" properties) can also be counted, and some good-making properties within the Form of the Good may be more important than others. Thus, the three kinds of goodness fall into a hierarchy of value (Edwards, 2010, 39-40). In application, since "better" means "more," people and other conscious individuals are better or more valuable than merely inanimate things, and mere things are better or more valuable than mere ideas or thoughts of things or of people (40-41).

Expressed abstractly, *intrinsically valuable entities have more goodness than extrinsically valuable entities because they have more good-making properties, and extrinsically valuable entities have more goodness than systemically valuable entities because they have more good-making properties.*

In application, this means that *people and other conscious beings have more value, more good-making properties, than useful but inanimate sensory objects and processes, and useful inanimate sensory objects and processes have more value, more good-making properties, than mere ideas of them or of people.* Also, *by degrees if not in kind,* people have more good-making properties than animals, and animals more than vegetables, and vegetables more than cells, and cells more than atoms, and atoms more than neutrons. Understanding "better" as "richer in good-making properties," axiology accounts for a hierarchy of worth in the three dimensions of goodness. It also allows for an axiological ranking of the natural kinds that Whitehead identified. Individuals belonging anywhere in Whitehead's natural hierarchy of importance may exemplify degrees or diverse instances of three varieties of axiological goodness. Capacities for actualizing them may vary significantly from species to species and between individuals within species. What counts as relevant good-making properties may also vary with the value sensitivities of rankers.

This axiological hierarchy of goodness may seem implausible initially, but it can be defended successfully. Placing the *least valuable of all, systemic values,* at the bottom of this hierarchy does not mean that ideas and beliefs have no value, or even very little value. Some good things can be very good, yet other good things can be even better. Systemic values—concepts, ideas, rules, beliefs, formal systems, etc.—are only mental symbols or tokens that point toward or apply to even more valuable realities. They have symbolic reference and point toward even better things than themselves (or sometimes to bad things). The idea of a close friend is very good, but a really close friend is even better. Fictions may be created with words and ideas, but the primary purpose of symbols is to point or refer to realities beyond themselves. We have words for or thoughts about people and mere things, but real people are more valuable than (have more good-making properties than) the verbal or abstract symbols that point to them. This is also true of desirable inanimate things, of useful sensory aggregates or physical processes, activities, and objects. A good car is more desirable than the mere idea of a good car. Physical entities and human activities can be very useful as means to ends beyond themselves; so they are more valuable than our words for, thoughts about, or conceptual symbols for them. We can spend the coins in our pockets, but we cannot spend our thoughts about those coins. Money in the bank is worth more than money that exists only in our minds or dreams, even if the two are numerically identical in face value and share other good-making descriptive properties. Real moral actions are more valuable than merely thinking about doing good and avoiding harm. Purely conceptual constructs fulfill only their definitional properties, but other kinds of goodness are richer in desirable properties.

Why are people more valuable than merely inanimate physical aggregates? In a nutshell, people are animate, conscious, and self-and-other valuing; but cars, houses, clothes, cash, coins, jewels, etc. are not. People have many good-making properties that inanimate but useful objects do not have. Real people are also worth more than all the thoughts we can think about them. Real friends and loved ones are worth more than all our ideas, truths, and beliefs about them. So is a real God. In relation to non-conscious systemic and extrinsic goods, mere thoughts and things, they are priceless.

VALUE COMBINATIONS AND CONFUSIONS

Regrettably, current process ethics has neither a well-developed hierarchy of value nor a theory of value combinations. Values may be combined as well as ranked. Beauty, as defined by Hartshorne, is an obvious value combination, consisting of just the right proportions of unity, diversity, complexity, and simplicity. But what is the value of a great work of art compared with the value of our thoughts and beliefs about it, or with the souls that created or enjoy it? What is the comparative worth of a desirable but unactualized eternal object and the same eternal object actualized or ingressed concretely into the actual world? The axiological hierarchy of value answers that question.

Next, how should we understand and deal with combinations of value? Value objects belonging to our three kinds or dimensions of goodness may be united or combined with one another in positive or negative, helpful or hurtful, value-increasing or value-decreasing ways. Hartman called positive value combinations "compositions" and negative combinations "transpositions" (1967, 268-80). Such value combinations may be organic wholes that are more valuable than the mere sum of their components. For example, we can use ideas to create useful products, and we can create and give useful or physically beautiful or interesting things to our friends and loved ones. People can unite with other people in marriage, family, companionship, and friendship. Houses can be bought or built for people, and depth of living within them can turn them into homes. Good ideas and positive beliefs can help us to become more thoughtful of and affectionate toward those we love, or more useful and helpful to our employers or employees. Examples of desirable value combinations are practically inexhaustible in number. Things that are otherwise good taken singly may also be combined with other good things in hurtful or destructive ways, e.g., when two good family sedans crash to make good junkers, or when one person kills another. Good ideas, useful things, and active people can be used to hurt people, destroy property, and degrade beliefs. Things that are otherwise good can enter into very undesirable value combinations.

Value combinations do not necessarily have the same worth as their component dimensions taken singly or additively. Great confusion may result when the values of wholes or parts are mistakenly identified. For example, when considering the value of systemically good things, intellectuals and dogmatists may be very partial to systemic goods without fully understanding why. They may confuse the value of ideas or other systemic goods with the much more valuable objects, individuals, or combinations they symbolize. They might think that knowledge is to be pursued for its own sake. They might believe that ideas are more valuable than mere things because they can do so much more with them. Well, which ideas, and which things? Good ideas plus their desirable consequences are rich combinations of value-objects in two or more dimensions, and that combination (ideas plus what we can do with them) should not be confused or identified with the value of the ideas alone.

To avoid such confusions, when assessing the relative worth of ideas and what they symbolize, follow this rule: Conceptual symbols must always be correlated only with the good things to which they refer (Edwards 2010, 48). Thus, we should not ask if *ideas in general* are not more valuable than cars, houses, lands, property, or people. We should ask instead if a real car is not more valuable than the mere idea of a car, if a real house is not better than the mere idea of a house, if real land and property are not worth more than the mere thoughts of such, if a real friend is not more valuable than the mere thought of one, and so on. Finally, we should ask if the value combination—the reality of a good idea *and* what we can do with it—is not more valuable than the mere thought of "a good idea and what we can do with it." The obvious answer to this question is, "Yes."

VALUATIONS, OR HOW WE VALUE

Three axiological ways of valuing correspond with our three basic kinds of goodness, and they are also called systemic, extrinsic, and intrinsic. Whitehead made much of how actual entities prehend other things. Prehension involves taking things into oneself and then processing and valuing them, but there are at least three basic axiological ways of prehending, as explained in what follows. This will add considerable clarity and depth to what Whitehead himself had to say about valuation. Whitehead gave some thought to *how* we and other actual entities value, that is, to the evaluation process, but much more needs to be said. A Hartmanian account of valuation can greatly advance process ethics, given its current state of development. Acknowledging that he focused mainly on valuations by fleeting actual occasions, not by enduring human souls, what did Whitehead say about valuation?

Whitehead thought that all actual entities or actual occasions are both valuing and valuable. He equated actuality with value/valuation, claiming that "An entity is actual, when it has significance for itself" (*PR*

25). Valuation is the essence of the subjective form of every conceptual feeling (*PR* 248). Valuation assesses and selects possibilities (pure eternal objects) to be actualized, or not. Whitehead emphasized the difference between positive and negative valuation (disvaluation). He referred to positive valuation as "valuation up" and "adversion," and to disvaluation as "valuation down" and "aversion" (*PR* 24, 234, 241, 247-48, 254, 276-77, 291), but he did not tell us when adversion and aversion are ethically appropriate or inappropriate. We ought to be averse to evils and adverse to aversions to evils, so value combinations can get very complicated. In one essay, Whitehead explicitly distinguished between "valuation" and "evaluation" (*SP* 88, 89). To make his long story short, valuation is the internal *conceptual activity* of making value judgments. Evaluation involves judgments, but it is primarily a matter of *affective responses and activities* requiring "a modification of events in time" (*SP* 89). Whitehead though that "All patterns of behaviour are in the long run sustained or modified by patterns of emotion and patterns of belief. It is the primary business of religion to concentrate upon emotion and belief" (*AI* 171). Of course, ethics and all axiological disciplines also focus upon emotion and belief, but this needs further analysis.

In this book, both the conceptual and the affective aspects of how we value are bundled together under the concept of "valuation." Valuation (or evaluation) involves conceptual ideals, what Whitehead called "initial aims" and "subjective aims," as well as affective processing, and it calls for behaviors that modify events in time. Subjective aims or ideals are initially supplied by God to every nascent occasion, but each must then decide what to do with them. Whitehead did not know about axiology's three dimensions of value and valuation, so he made no effort to show which ideals and feelings are most appropriate for particular value dimensions or combinations. Formal axiology adds considerable axiological insight and clarity to what Whitehead had to say about how we value.

So what worthwhile insights can formal axiology add to Whitehead's account of how we value? For one thing, it gives a much more illuminating account of how real people or enduring souls value, as opposed to fleeting actual occasions. Also, it explains that good things, value-objects, data evaluated, exist within *three value dimensions*—systemic, extrinsic, and intrinsic. They are *what* we value. *How* we value is equally important, though often neglected by philosophers of every description (Edwards 2010, Ch. 3). Formal axiology explains *how we are supposed to value, how it would be best to value,* in each value dimension, even if other ways also have positive value.

How we value involves *both thoughts and feelings.* Some philosophers assume that valuing involves thoughts alone (Kant, Moore), others that valuing involves feelings alone (subjectivists, emotivists, and logical positivists). Both groups capture only half the truth. The whole truth, says formal axiology, is that valuing properly involves both thoughts and feelings that are expressed in acting in due time. Valuation is a rational and affective process that calls for action, just as Whitehead said.

Mentally or rationally, evaluating value-objects of all three kinds (and their combinations) involves creating, refining, and applying relevant standards—ideal sets of good-making properties appropriate for each value kind, then gaining knowledge of the actual properties of value-objects, then matching ideal with actual properties to determine degrees of correlation. Do the valued objects really exemplify their ideal properties, and to what degree?

Affectively, value-objects are evaluated through different kinds and degrees of feeling. Whitehead recognized this in a very general way, writing, "Importance reveals itself as transitions of emotion" (*MT* 117).

He emphasized the feeling of enjoyment and affirmed of every actual occasion, "The aim is at the enjoyment belonging to the process" (*MT* 152). This makes him sound like a hedonist, except that enjoyment was not the only thing he valued intensely. He rightly recognized intensity of feeling or emotion as a key element in valuation, but he gave little attention to degrees of it, or to how feelings do or should correlate with different kinds of value.

Formal axiology provides a more careful analysis of the kinds and degrees of feeling, affection, desires, emotions, etc. involved in human evaluation. Different intensities of feeling belong most naturally and appropriately with value-objects (Whitehead's "data") in different value dimensions. Ideally, degrees of valuation should be proportioned to degrees of value. That would be the best way to do it. The least valuable things should normally be valued with the least passion or intensity, the most with the most intensity, and those in between more moderately. Good things with the most value (intrinsic values) should normally be valued with strongest feelings and commitments, those with less value (extrinsic values) with less intensity of feeling and commitment, and those with the least value (systemic values) with the least intensity of feeling and commitment.

Most appropriately, we should be most intensely and decisively involved with persons or conscious beings through feelings of love, compassion, and self-identification (intrinsic valuation). We should intensely delight in them and rejoice in their presence and existence. The Stoics were wrong in thinking we should value even those closest to us in life only disinterestedly or uninterestedly, i.e., that we should not be emotionally involved with them. The Stoics did not have the courage to love. The courage to love is a good-making property of a truly abundant human life.

We should be involved less intensely, passionately, and decisively with mere things or mindless aggregates. "Materialistic" people overvalue them and "go overboard" for them. Ordinary everyday practical desires and feelings manifest extrinsic evaluation.

We should be involved even less intensely and more dispassionately, objectively, or disinterestedly (but not uninterestedly) with symbols, ideas, systems, rules, regulations, and beliefs (systemic evaluation).

Degrees of affective involvement and moral development shade off gradually into one another, but hard core instances of these three are identifiable. Systemic evaluation is the least intense kind of affective involvement, but it is not mere indifference or uninterestedness. Intrinsic evaluation is the most intense kind of affective involvement, and extrinsic evaluation falls somewhere in between. What philosophers call "approval" comes in many shades and varieties. Of course, there are complications, considered next.

VALUING GOOD THINGS IN DIFFERENT DIMENSIONS

Any value-object in any dimension can be evaluated as if it belongs to some other value dimension. The distinction between value-objects (*what* we value) and evaluations (*how* we value) is ethically relevant and important. Recall that "ought" means "This would be best, so do it." Ideally we ought to value intrinsic value objects intrinsically, extrinsic value objects extrinsically, and systemic value objects systemically, *but mixing them up is not always bad or unethical. Sometimes it is.*

Intellectuals generally, (e.g., philosophers, theologians, natural scientists, college professors), aspire to evaluate ideas, beliefs, rules and all systemically valuable conceptual constructs disinterestedly or objectively. So do courtroom judges. They strive to be rationally objective or impartial in dealing with their subject matter. Whitehead recognized that objectivity is not uninterestedness: "The most ardent upholders of objectivity in scientific thought insist upon its importance" (*MT* 8-9). Objectivity involves some degree of interest, passion, and feeling, but not so much as to cloud or distort fair-minded or impartial judgment.

Scholars do indeed have their low-intensity "objective" moments, but they often evaluate knowledge, truth, beliefs, and doctrines quite passionately, and they intensely relish the creative insight of "Aha" experiences. An attack upon their ideas may be experienced as a personal assault or affront. They may detest those who disagree with them. They can and often do evaluate systemic value-objects systemically or disinterestedly, but very often they evaluate them intrinsically, that is, quite passionately and lovingly. They may personally identify themselves very intensely with their chosen or inherited ideas, methodologies, and beliefs. Whitehead noted that the great Indian mathematician, Ramanujan, took great "delight" in numbers and mathematical insights: "It was said of him that each of the first hundred integers was his personal friend" (*MT* 47). He personified and intrinsically evaluated numbers. Hartman said that in intrinsic valuation, even a thing or a thought "becomes a Self identified with the valuing Self, a Thou to the I" (1994, 98). Numbers may be evaluated as if they were people, but they cannot love us back! Yet, numbers have no souls of their own, no capacity for self-enjoyment, no ability to reciprocate love, no intrinsic worth.

Nothing is wrong with evaluating non-intrinsic values *intrinsically as long as the fundamental hierarchy of value remains intact,* and we love good things in proportion to their true worth. This is important where values in different dimensions come into conflict. Political authoritarians, intellectual snobs, and philosophical, theological, and scientific dogmatists may intensely disvalue people who do not conform to or accept their thoughts, doctrines, methods, and beliefs. They may systemically disvalue intrinsic values. They may go much further. They may intensely overvalue systemic values that lack souls and undervalue intrinsic values with souls. They may intensely disvalue those intrinsically valuable human beings who do not accept or at least conform to their thoughts, beliefs, dogmas, ideologies, and formalities. Even if they do not disvalue their students, some college professors may love them less than they love ideas, truth, or knowledge and act accordingly. An intense attachment to systemic values at the expense of intrinsic values is unethical.

But what if ideas and people are both loved? There is nothing wrong with loving numbers, as did Ramanujan, as long as this love is accompanied by an adequate and proportionate love of and respect for self, other persons, and other ensouled actualities. How did his intrinsic passion for mathematics affect the rest of Ramanujan's life? How competent was he in managing his practical affairs, including his own body, health, work, and wealth? How much involvement with and love for other people did he have? Was his intrinsic evaluation of systemic values an overvaluation at the expense of extrinsic practical values and/or of intrinsic interpersonal values? Was his personality developed in all dimensions of goodness, or was he an axiologically astigmatized or warped person? Could he manage his own practical affairs? Was he good at his job? Did he treat everyone with respect and at least some with great affection? Did he have adequate intimate personal relations with friends and loved ones? Was he adequately developed in all dimensions of value and evaluation?

Numbers as well as philosophical, theological, and scientific ideas may be loved at the expense of souls, but not necessarily so. Systemic values may be ranked over intrinsic values. Socrates displayed this propensity when he insisted that the philosophically unexamined life is not worth living. Many intellectual snobs take the same "value down" or "aversive" stance toward non-intellectuals. Yet, non-intellectuals who are weak (but never totally undeveloped) systemically may nevertheless have very rich and worthwhile ordinary lives filled with countless creative practical values and competencies. They may also be very rich in moral or spiritual goodness, immensely helpful to others, filled with creative love, compassion, devotion, and other profound moral and spiritual virtues, and very active in expressing these virtues in the real world. Their unexamined lives are very much worth living!

VALUING MERE THINGS IN THREE DIMENSIONS

Now consider how we might value mere things (inanimate sense objects or aggregates) like knives, tables, newspapers, and artistic creations in three dimensions. How should and how can we relate to them? Obviously, they have no consciousness or awareness of their own and no systemic, extrinsic, or intrinsic values or evaluation capacities of their own. Clearly, they have no intrinsic value. They are nothing more than extrinsically or practically useful value-objects. We can still value them in three different ways, systemically, extrinsically, and intrinsically. We can do the same with systemic value-objects like knowledge or beliefs, and with intrinsic value objects like people and animals. We can value any value-object in any value dimension as if it belongs to some other value dimension. We often do, and this is not always unethical.

Evaluation in all three dimensions has two components, a conceptual or rational component (concept fulfillment) and an affective component (our emotional or affective involvement).

Consider a pocket knife as an example. In itself, a pocket knife is simply an extrinsically valuable (useful) perceptual object or tool, but we may relate to it evaluationally in three distinctive ways.

Evaluating a knife or any extrinsic value object *systemically* involves both intellect and minimal affections or feelings. (1) Rationally, we do this by applying only a few abstract Form of the Good predicates to it. Do its actual properties actually fulfill its purely formal predicates? Does it exemplify the definitional properties of "knife"? (It might be only a rubber or plastic toy that will not cut anything.) Does it have the mathematical and geometrical properties of a good pocket knife? (A poorly manufactured one may not.) (2) Affectively, we can relate to these minimal formal properties only objectively or disinterestedly, with minimal interests, but not uninterestedly.

We can also evaluate pocket knives either extrinsically or intrinsically. Evaluating a knife or any extrinsic value object *extrinsically* also involves both reason and affections. (1) Rationally, we can apply a more complex Form of the Good to it. Do its actual properties actually fulfill some richer set of ideal expositional predicates? A good pocket knife can be used for cutting, chopping, and defending. How well do the properties of this particular knife fulfill the expectations of usefulness that we have for it? Does it actually have the good-making expositional properties that it ought to have? Is this knife worth its weight in gold? Even gold is merely an extrinsic value object, highly prized for its immense utility. Precise quantities of it can also be numbered in weight and cash value, so it can be combined with systemic values. (2) Affectively, we can relate to the usefulness of knives and gold through our normal everyday practical desires, feelings, attitudes, and interests without "going overboard" and overvaluing it. We may decide that we ought to take good care of this knife simply because of its usefulness.

Evaluating a knife or any extrinsic value object *intrinsically* also involves both reason and affections. (1) Rationally, we can apply an even more complex Form of the Good to it. Do its actual properties actually fulfill an even richer set of ideal predicates? We can conceptually consider a pocket knife in its full uniqueness, definiteness, and completeness. How does it differ from all other knives in the universe? What are its individuating properties? Does it have any psychological properties? Why do we find it especially appealing? Do we have any unique personal relations with it? Is it a beautiful thing? (2) Affectively, we can relate to it with profound sensitivity, love, affection, delight, and personal identification, as if it were person-like, as if it were an old friend. When affectively evaluating them intrinsically, we typically associate or psychologically combine extrinsic value objects, mere things, with persons.

Intrinsic evaluations of extrinsic sensory objects may be value compositions, not simple evaluations of inanimate objects as such. For example, we may intensely value this particular pocket knife because it belonged to our father or grandfather, who we recall with great affection. Perhaps we remember using it ourselves on a wonderful camping trip with our own children. Thereby, we personally identify intensely with this particular knife/grandfather, or with that special knife/camping trip with-our-children. There is a very real axiological and psychological difference between the value of a *mere* pocket knife and *my grandfather's* pocket knife.

Misers might intensely and directly value "for its own sake" the gold or money that the knife is worth. They might create their own personal identities around it, without further associations. However, most people value gold, money, or wealth in any form extrinsically, i.e., for what we can do with it, for its usefulness in getting other things that we want. We easily recognize that misers overvalue gold or cash.

No matter how we value it, a pocket knife as such is just a pocket knife, a physical object with no mind, awareness, consciousness, thoughts, sensitivity, feelings, or values of its own. No amount of value-association, reflection, or emotion can ever get around that brute fact. This must also be said of tables, chairs, newspapers, and physical works of art. A newspaper is inherently a value compound or composition, being both a physical object and a locus of systemic thoughts, ideas, beliefs, and information. We can separate these two elements and consider a newspaper merely as useful kitty litter, or we can ignore its physicality and consider only the thoughts and news it brings to mind.

Even professional axiologists may not be mindful of the distinction, or they may confuse values (what we value) with evaluations (how we value), so don't be discouraged if you share this confusion. Robert S. Hartman himself sometimes called art-objects like beautiful paintings and sculptures "intrinsic values," though surely he meant only that we can evaluate them intrinsically. We often think and feel that way about beautiful paintings, sculptures, and other works of art. Strictly speaking, they are only extrinsic value-objects, even in their glorious beauty, concreteness, and uniqueness, and even when we evaluate them intrinsically with profound positive feelings. A beautiful statue by Michelangelo has no mind, awareness, consciousness, thoughts, sensitivity, feelings, or values of its own. It has no soul. It is not intrinsically good. It is not an end in, to, and for itself, but we can still profoundly identify with it aesthetically and speak metaphorically of its "intrinsic value." Yet, this is metaphorical speech.

Often, evaluating value-objects in some other dimension is a very good thing that enhances overall value. Sometimes it is not, most obviously when this diminishes the value of something good. Overvaluation or undervaluation are comparative. They involve valuing things as if they were something else and ranking them wrongly in relation to other better or less valuable value-objects. This can have great ethical significance. For example, people can be evaluated as if they were mere things or property (as slaves, or as nothing more than expendable workers or "hands"), or as if they were mere tokens or ciphers in a system (as in all forms of ideology and dogmatism).

Animals are often valued only for their utility or cash value as meat producing factories, and they are treated accordingly. Animals, especially our pets, are sometimes selectively valued intrinsically. This is often said to be their "sentimental value," as opposed to their "real" monetary or utility value. Objectively, all animals and not just pets have such sentimental value (intrinsic worth), though we do not always see it (evaluate them intrinsically). Things and beliefs can be valued passionately as if they were persons, and persons may be valued as mere things, or as merely systemic tokens in ideological systems. Most of the moral evils of human existence involve either undervaluing people and animals, or outright disvaluing them.

Nothing is inherently wrong with positively, passionately, and intensely (intrinsically) evaluating everything in any value dimension as long as the hierarchy of value is sustained, that is, as long as value-objects are loved in proportion to their actual degree of goodness, as specified in the axiological hierarchy of value. All things may be loved without being unethical, but only in proportion to their true worth relative to other good things, especially when they are in conflict. This is the way that the saints value in every culture, but most of us fall far short of saintliness (Edwards 2010, 125-30).

5.

DEGREES, ETHICS, AND VIRTUE

As most process ethicists have done, this chapter recognizes degrees of intrinsic goodness and explores the relevance of this to so called "marginal cases" and to our ethical relations with animals and other living things. Then it develops additional moral themes that are underdeveloped in the present state of process ethics. It offers a three-dimensional understanding of ethics itself and of the moral virtues that belong within an expanded axiological process ethics. It identifies some major obstacles to living ethically, and it shows how optimally developed morality merges into spirituality.

DEGREES OF INTRINSIC WORTH, MARGINAL CASES, AND ANIMALS

All normal human beings share the five basic defining properties of intrinsic worth developed in Chapter Two. Because we do, we are entitled to basic human or intrinsic value rights, not only to life, liberty, and the pursuit of happiness, but also to die and marry as we choose, and to many other entitlements. However, not all people, and not all living things, share these five properties equally. They come in degrees. Also, our overall well-being is not the same thing as our intrinsic worth. We do not all have equal shares of the well-being-making properties that contribute to the overall abundance or goodness of human and non-human life. We do not all lead equally good lives, morally or otherwise. Normal human beings are minimally equal but not maximally equal in intrinsic-good-making properties, and people are very unequal in quality of life properties. *There are degrees of intrinsic worth and degrees of overall well-being, not only between but also within species.*

Not all intrinsically valuable actual entities are of equal worth. All normal human beings meet the minimum requirements and should be afforded equal rights. With respect to well-being, however, some people clearly live better or more abundant-in-goodness lives than others, lives much richer in positive quality of life enrichment properties. Some but not all of these are moral properties. The cruelties and injustices of the natural world and of other people deny equal opportunities for self-development, self-creativity, self-expression, and self-realization to many people. Ethics has something to say about this, much to say, as a matter of fact. Some people just do not take advantage of the opportunities they have. Some just make self-defeating decisions intellectually, practically, socially, affectively, morally, and spiritually. Many are defeated by their physical, social, and economic circumstances and by the moral failures of others. Often we as individuals do not fulfill the broad evaluational standards that we set for ourselves, or those supported by axiological process ethics. When measured by the Form of the Good, we fall short morally and in many other ways.

Atoms, animals, and people, Whitehead insisted, meet the minimal requirement (self-significance), but not all intrinsically valuable actualities have either equally intrinsic or maximal valuable or desirable lives. If this were not so, we would never have any ethical problems! This is both obvious and significant when considering ontological or biological species and their comparative intrinsic worth. To understand such differences, we must apply the Form of the Good comparatively to electrons, atoms, molecules, cells, plants, animals, and people. What are their good-making properties, and what do they lack? Are all equally self-significant, self- and others- valuing, conscious or aware, enduring, numerically individuated, and unique? Some are barely if at all conscious or unique. Electrons, atoms, molecules, etc. are numerically individuated, but they have very few distinctively individuating properties other than their indefinite spatiotemporal locations and the minute spontaneous "swerving," unpredictability, indefiniteness, and discontinuities allowed to them by the Heisenberg Uncertainty Principle and quantum physics.

Whitehead saw very little creativity, diversity, awareness, or uniqueness in low-grade organisms: "The low-grade organism is merely the summation of the forms of energy which flow in upon it in all their multiplicity of detail. It receives, it transmits; but it fails to simplify into intelligible system" (*PR* 254). The unique spatiotemporal locus of atoms and sub-atomic particles and waves is anything but the "simple location" in absolute time and space of classical Newtonian physics (*SMW,* 49, 58, 71). It is only the indefinite location allowed to them by relativity and quantum physics. Atoms and electrons mainly just reiterate their type-patterns over and over again.

Some physical and biological kinds differ only in *degrees* of our five intrinsic value definitional properties, but often the differences are in richness of *additional well-being-making properties.* According to Whitehead, "When we turn to the lower organisms we have first to determine which among such capacities fade from realization into irrelevance, that is to say, by comparison with human experience which is our standard" (*PR* 112). Some intrinsically good entities are more complex than others, but this is not mere theoretical complexity in the abstract. Rather, some actually existing entities manifest a vast array of positive desirable qualities (ingressed eternal objects) that others do not exemplify.

Cells have good-making properties that electrons and atoms do not have; plants have good-making properties that cells do not have; animals have good-making properties that plants do not have; people have good-making properties that *many* animals do not have, though some of our differences from animals like Bonobo chimps are mainly in degree. Yet, degrees can be very significant. Among animals, including rational animals, there are noteworthy differences in good-making properties, both degree and kind. Mice *probably* live richer-in-goodness lives than jellyfish and fleas, beavers than mice (if for no other reason than that they live about eight times as long), deer than beavers, great apes and porpoises than deer, most people than great apes and porpoises. Normal people typically have better lives than severely retarded or irreversibly comatose human beings. These details remain to be sorted out. Much work has been done on natural hierarchies, but much work remains to be done in the areas of marginal cases and comparative inter-species ethics and evaluations using the Form of the Good.

Degrees of intrinsic goodness give rise inevitably to many vexing issues, covered largely by the troublesome ethical category of "marginal cases." Even on the human biological level, there are significant differences in degrees of intrinsic worth. Fortunately, the most significant differences are uncommon. Biologically human organisms who are severely retarded, comatose, or in a permanent vegetative state either fail to exemplify the most essential of the five defining properties of intrinsic worth, or else they do so only to an exceptionally small degree. This brute fact cannot be swept under the table. Yet, making accurate judgments about degrees of intrinsic worth is so difficult and susceptible to corruption that whenever possible, we should always give the benefit of the doubt when ascribing and respecting basic moral rights. Due to our own perversity, self-deception, and fallibility, judging the worth of others can be very dangerous, but sometimes in extreme marginal cases we have to judge. Conflicts of rights and degrees of intrinsic worth among intrinsically valuable beings create very real and unavoidable moral problems in medical and veterinary ethics, where there are many honest disagreements. Consider a few examples.

ABORTION

In the hot topic of *abortion,* issues are framed conceptually in a variety of ways (Edwards and Graber 1988, Ch. 8; Cobb 1991, Ch. 3), and often with very little clarity or relevance. Conservatives say that one-celled neo-conceptuses ("the moment of conception") are full "human beings," or "persons," or "alive," and are thus entitled to all human rights, including the right to life, which should protect them from being aborted, even when they are the product of rape or incest. This raises the issues about how such concepts are to be understood, whether our definitions are actually being fulfilled, and whether these concepts are really relevant. What exactly are the defining properties of "human beings," or "persons," or "life," and how do these properties relate to our five defining properties of "intrinsic value"?

Being "alive" and "having a beating heart" cannot define human beings or persons, for almost all mammals, fish, snakes, and other animals are alive and have beating hearts. Human egg and sperm cells are not dead before they unite, and they are human. They are alive, so when does *life* begin? About five billion years ago. And when does *human (Homo sapiens)* life begin? About two hundred thousand years ago. Most importantly, being human, being alive, or having a beating heart are not among the five defining properties of "intrinsic value." These concepts are really quite irrelevant to the abortion controversy.

The really crucial ethical issue in all marginal cases is the presence or absence of degrees of intrinsic worth. Dealing with this issue requires clear thinking, relevant information, and applying the Form of the Good. In the abortion controversy, the most basic intrinsic value property is consciousness or awareness. Without that, there can be no valuation of self or anything else. Self- and other-valuation depend on that, but when do developing embryos or fetuses manifest wakeful evaluative awareness or consciousness? Certainly not at conception, and not when they develop beating and pumping hearts at around four to six weeks after conception. Brain waves indicative of a wakeful soul field are not present in developing fetuses until somewhere between weeks 25 and 27 of pregnancy, that is, near or at the beginning of the "third trimester." This is the earliest we can say that they are ensouled with valuing consciousness or awareness. This is also the earliest that they can consciously experience pain, though they may earlier manifest reflex responses to pain stimuli. This is when they begin to manifest the most essential and distinctive properties of intrinsic worth. But even this is only a primitive beginning. Becoming a person is a developmental process (Edwards and Graber, 529-33ff). Even the "moment of conception" is a process that takes time. It is much more than a "moment."

Conflicting rights are present in various ways in the abortion controversy. *Rights morally, legally, or socially protect unique intrinsically valuable beings against very basic harms, or entitle them to very basic goods.* In abortion situations, the rights of two intrinsically valuable beings come into conflict, the right of the fetus to life (which kicks in at some controversial point in its development) and the right of the mother to decide what to do with her own body and to kill if necessary in self-defense. Continuing a pregnancy and protecting the life of the fetus sometimes seriously jeopardize the life and health of the mother. Widely accepted in practice is the view that the mother's rights should prevail because her intrinsic value properties are much more developed than those of the fetus, and partly because her already established social relations, which the fetus largely lacks, count heavily in her favor. Also, only the potential mother is actually capable of making such choices at all, and only she and those who know and love her can and must face the anxieties and liabilities of her possible death and loss. Where will the least harm be done when such tough choices must be made?

If religious convictions get involved, anti-abortion conservatives have the right to practice their faith themselves and in their own consenting families, but they do not have the right to impose their theology of abortion on others who sincerely disagree. Many conservatives insist that a "baby" receives its immortal soul at the "moment of conception," but religious authorities differ significantly among themselves about this and have disagreed about it for centuries. Even if it is granted that all abortions are evil and undesirable, we still have to choose at times between the lesser of two evils.

Empirically, what exactly does a single cell neo-conceptus have that its "parent" egg and sperm cell did not have before they united? Answer: A complete set of human genes. Both the ovum and sperm had only half a set. So is everything with a complete set of human genes a living person? Surely not, for every cell in our bodies has a complete set of human genes, except for red blood cells. Is it "murder" to kill anything that has a complete set of human genes? If so, then it is murder to destroy almost any human cell. Since almost any human cell can now be cloned to make a baby, all human cells are "potential persons." Weighing information, relevant facts, consequences, and rights is no easy matter in marginal cases, especially so with respect to abortions, so honest disagreements are predictable, and compromises that leave no one perfectly satisfied are inevitable. Where controversy is intense, and so many relevant considerations are uncertain, as much freedom of choice as possible should be allowed socially, legally, and morally. The *Roe v. Wade* decision of 1973 seems to be a workable abortion compromise with respect to what should be thus permitted. Morally, both conservatives and their opponents should be able to agree on many "better than" judgments. For example: it is better to use contraception than to conceive and abort; it is better to abort earlier in pregnancy than later; adoption is better than abortion if this is acceptable to the pregnant woman all things considered, finding common ground is better than vilifying, and perhaps many more.

TERMINAL CASES

Marginal *end-of-life* ethical problems are very similar to marginal beginning of life problems (Edwards and Graber, 1988, Ch. 7; Cobb 1991, Ch. 2). At some point, we will all be ready to go, despite our intrinsic worth—or we will go ready or not. Ethically, we have moral duties to ourselves as well as to others, and we prefer to have some say-so about how we will die if and when this is possible. We execute living wills and select trusted proxy decision makers to carry out our end of life wishes. We may also have to decide how and when to let our loved ones go, despite their intrinsic worth and our great devotion to them. We may find ourselves making end of life decisions not just for ourselves but for those loved ones or friends who are irreversibly deprived of all intrinsic goodness (comatose) or else overwhelmed by insufferable suffering.

End of life ethical dilemmas arise in situations of insufferable and unrelievable painful consciousness, irreversible marginal consciousness, or no consciousness at all. What would we choose for ourselves or our loved ones if lapsed irreversibly into a persistent vegetative state where sleep/wake cycles are present, but there is little or no awareness of or responsiveness to anything? What would we choose if we or our loved ones are in a much deeper and irreversible coma with no sleep/wake cycles, little or no upper brain activity, and no awareness of or responsiveness to anything? Here all the central defining properties of intrinsic worth are gone. What does it mean to treat persons as ends and not merely as means when death is either immanent and unavoidable, or else highly desirable as the lesser of evils, all things considered? When we are competent to decide or have left advance directives, it means allowing us to make this decision for ourselves without hindrance from laws, relatives, doctors, or others who disagree. Where self-directives are unavailable and patients are either incompetent to decide or too immature to understand, choices must by made by others on the basis of what is in that person's best interests. In all such cases, past or high intrinsic worth should not be confused with present intrinsic worth, which may be absent.

UNRELIEVABLE SUFFERING

What about unendurable situations in which we no longer value ourselves or much of anything else, situations in which normal consciousness and self-valuation prospects afford little else than *unrelievable excruciating pains,* whether mental, physical, or both? Some theorists say that there is nothing bad about pain because it is a natural and useful indicator of problems that need to be corrected, but no one who is actually in excruciating pain would believe that, and suffering is often way out of proportion to serving that goal. Presumably, such theorists would sense no ethical obligation to prevent or relieve great pain, or have any moral scruples against inflicting it, but that would be quite unethical.

Also, no one in a state of great and unrelievable suffering would ever be convinced that evil is mere privation of goodness. Being irreversibly comatose is privation of intrinsic worth, but immense suffering for which there is no relief is a demonic presence, not an absence or a privation. Fortunately, medicine has made great advances in providing pain-relief, but this often involves loss of consciousness and even of life. Also, these methods do not always work, they are not fool-proof, and legal barriers often inhibit their use. *In some situations evil and ugliness are so real and potent that we are no longer self-valuing souls.* Then we no longer have intrinsic worth in the sense that we no longer positively value our continued existence at the price of and in the presence of such overwhelming and unrelievable suffering. We look upon death as a blessing, not a curse.

Then, we should be allowed to choose death either actively or passively by "killing," "assisted suicide," or "letting die." "Active means" involve performing some act that hastens death; "passive means" involve withholding or withdrawing all "artificial" or "extraordinary" means of life support while continuing to provide whatever is necessary for comfort and pain relief. The line between the two is not crystal clear, for "pulling the plug" is an act, providing means to pain relief may hasten death, and at some point all methods of life support become "extraordinary means." Who should pull the plug or administer pain-relieving drugs that might be lethal? Must it be the patients themselves, or might others assist? Why not either or both? The very meaning of "death" is uncertain, and definitions may vary significantly from state to state (Edwards and Graber 388-391). In our living wills or through our proxies, we should be allowed to choose both a "good death," and what counts as "death."

Where suffering is a major consideration, the rationale for using active means to bring about the death of those who choose it is exactly the same as that for using passive means. What is that rationale?

1. It prevents pointless, intense, and unrelievable pain.

2. It does not violate their rights since they voluntarily waive their right to life.

3. It respects their autonomy, their right to choose a "good death" for themselves.

4. They do not believe that suffering that serves no other purpose is good for the soul.

5. It conforms to the Golden Rule.

6. It is often in the best interests not only of the patients themselves but of others, for example, family members who are being excessively burdened, or potential organ and tissue recipients.

Here "best interests" and "good death" need not be something obviously positive; they are the lesser of all the evils.

ANIMALS

Ethical concerns about marginal cases, degrees of intrinsic worth, and insurmountable suffering also extend deeply into the *sub-human world*. We do not always view them that way, but animals also fulfill our five defining criteria of intrinsic worth. Many process thinkers have written significantly about our ethical relations with animals (Dombrowski 1988, 1997; Cobb 1991, Ch. 1; Edwards 1995, Henning 12-22, 163-72). How do we ethically justify experimenting on intrinsically valuable animals? Do degrees of harm or of intrinsic worth count? Do the purposes of such experiments count, for example, commercial versus medical rationales? Have viable alternatives been adequately considered?

Can we ethically justify raising and killing unique, self- and other-valuing, conscious, animals for food? Vegetarians are not convinced by the usual reasons given to justify raising, killing, and eating animals. It is often argued that we give pigs, cows, chickens, turkeys, and other domestic animals a good life for a short amount of time that they would not otherwise have if we were not raising them for food. A big part of the problem with this "Blessed is the pig for the Englishman is fond of bacon" argument is that given today's factory farming methods, most of the animals we eat live miserable lives, not good lives, before being killed for food, and most of them die in great terror and pain. Also, we would not consent to raising human infants for food on the same grounds, that is, because we could thereby give them a good life for a short time that they would not otherwise have.

Whitehead's "life is robbery" (*PR* 105) cannot be used to justify much more than vegetarianism. Even that is robbery, but, as Whitehead put it, "The robber requires justification" (105) *The life-robber is ethically bound to steal only the necessary minimum.* Some people think that killing animals for food is justified because we need animal food for health and survival, but vegetarians have effectively refuted that argument many times. Everything we human beings require for both adequate nutrition and gustatory enjoyment is available to us through plant foods, and this includes getting balanced proteins from mixed plant sources. Many vegetarian cookbooks are now available that tell us how to do this quite successfully. Yes, a few people like the Eskimos do not have access to plant foods, and since we have killed off all of the predators in many other places, we may have to kill some animals to prevent their overpopulation and starvation, or else reintroduce their predators (and thus kill them indirectly). Tough choices have to be made when nature is out of balance, especially when we have made it so.

Most of us do not have the "absolute necessity" excuse. In rare cases of real conflict, degrees of intrinsic worth favor the Eskimos over the caribou, seals, whales, fish, and other animals that they eat. If all living things have a right to life, the strength of that right varies with degrees of intrinsic worth. When choosing what to kill and eat, most of our lives are not at stake, and our right to life does not conflict with the pig's right to life. The only conflict is between our taste for meat and the animal's *life*. Our right to enjoy tasty food is not even at stake, for plant food can be made incredibly tasty when we take the trouble to learn how to cook properly. Our own lives and our whole environment would be immensely healthier if we live as vegetarians and rob only plants. Becoming a vegetarian is not easy for many people, and many of us sin against animals even though we know better. Vegetarianism is better than killing and eating animals (Dombrowski 1988, 1997). Raising and killing animals for food is not a trivial issue. Henning points out "that over 100 million cows, pigs, and sheep and over 5 billion chickens are raised and slaughtered annually in the United States alone" (168).

Returning to people, in marginal cases we differ from one another intrinsically by degrees as well as in richness of good making properties. Partly, this is because desirable experiences and activities add to our total property inventories over the course of time. With respect for "good for" properties, we differ by degrees, sometimes significantly, from most animals and plants. For example, our individual spiritual and moral capacities, development, actions, and virtues make a great difference. Many non-human animals have some moral virtues, such as being affectionate and capable parents, making self-sacrifices for others, engaging in many pro-social behaviors, and in some instances enforcing and following socially beneficial rules. As with most of us, animals usually apply these moral virtues only to insiders. The moral differences between them and us are not absolute, as philosophers and non-philosophers once thought; but differences in degree as well as kind are significant. Get out the Form of the Good and calculate!

INTRINSIC, MORAL, AND SPIRITUAL GOODNESS

"Intrinsically good," "morally good," and "spiritually good" are distinct concepts having different definitions. They can be independently fulfilled, even if they overlap for some purposes in meaning and symbolic reference. They include different good-making properties, and all can be used to measure actual people and their good-making properties. No normal person can fail to be intrinsically good; anyone can fail to be morally or spiritually good. Almost everyone fails morally and spiritually, some of us more than others.

Morally wicked people exemplify all of the definitional intrinsic-good-making properties that morally good people exemplify, and they have many other desirable qualities and personality traits. They are conscious, self-conscious, self-concerned, valuing, intelligent, affective, active, internally free, enduring, and unique. They have feelings and experiences that go far beyond self-enjoyment and self-evaluation. They make creative and responsible choices. They have values in every dimension, and they have a practically uncountable number properties that make them unique individuals. They are intrinsically good even when they are morally bad. They have moral rights even when they are morally bad. They are entitled to being protected by all human rights, at least up to the point where they forfeit them through gross immorality and illegality, or when they can no longer benefit from them.

Morality and spirituality, degrees of each, or the lack of each, are integral aspects of our uniqueness and well-being. Another very valuable (good for us) property is our *freedom to be either morally or spiritually good or morally or spiritually bad,* or to fall somewhere in between, by degrees. So how should an axiological process ethics deal with ethics itself, and with moral or ethical goodness and badness? Spirituality will come later.

THREE DIMENSIONS OF ETHICS AND VIRTUE

Ethics is understood by most philosophers to pertain to our relations with human beings, ourselves included. In recent decades especially, the range of ethics has been profoundly extended to include our relations with non-human animals and our wider natural environment. Since we exist in social orders, they are also ethically relevant. *Being ethical is a matter of relating to others (human and non-human) for the common good.* This means valuing, thinking, feeling, and acting to achieve the common good, and this includes preventing and not inflicting harms (bad-making properties). Ethics requires a knowledge of right and wrong, good and evil, and it imposes duties to teach and learn the differences between them. It is grounded affectively in positively valuing and caring about and for intrinsically valuable actual entities. "Moral" and "ethical" will serve as synonyms in this discussion. We will focus mainly on ethical relations between people, but please keep animals in mind as you read further. Applied ethics presupposes that people, animals, and perhaps other actual entities have intrinsic worth, are ends in themselves, and should be so regarded and treated.

Good-making moral motives and dispositions are commonly called "virtues," though there are also non-moral virtues, for example, the intellectual virtues of fair-mindedness, curiosity, insight, logical thinking, etc. Moral virtues are enduring dispositions to behave morally, that is, to think, feel, and act in ways that promote the common good. Aristotle suggested that morally right or correct actions are those that morally virtuous persons would do. What is now called "virtue ethics" springs from this insight. Process ethics has had little to say thus far about being and becoming morally virtuous. It would be difficult, though not impossible, to developed a process virtue ethics. Such issues have not been totally neglected, however, but more needs to be said. Identifying morally correct beliefs, thoughts, feelings, motives, and actions as those that virtuous people would have and do calls for understanding what morally good persons are like, and their virtues.

Formal axiology analyzes *ethics and virtues in three dimensions*. In real people these three dimensions are never cleanly separated. Simply stated, systemic virtues involve systemic valuation, extrinsic virtues involve extrinsic valuation, and intrinsic virtues involve intrinsic valuation. These fall into a hierarchy of value, and the higher stages include the lower. Many ethical theories are exclusively or at least primarily one dimensional and one sided. All three approaches to ethics may involve elements of the other two, but in each one ethical dimension is dominant over the others. For example, Kant's ethics was primarily formal, focused systemically on the moral law, but even that required extrinsic acting in accord with the law. Nothing about the following discussion is exhaustive.

SYSTEMIC ETHICS AND SYSTEMIC VIRTUES

Systemic ethics is expressed conceptually or rationally in formal moral systems, beliefs, rules, regulations, principles, rights, commandments, etc. Some ethical theories like that of Kant and other deontologists are primarily systemic in nature. Kant never got very far beyond the systemic. He deliberately excluded moral consequences, feelings, and desires from ethics, but even he required moral actions in accord with his moral imperatives. Formal axiology, by contrast, embraces beliefs, feelings, actions, and virtues in all three dimensions, systemic, extrinsic, and intrinsic and proceeds towards an inclusive intrinsic virtue ethics. Moral rules or guidelines may be approved, adopted, or affirmed systemically, dispassionately, or objectively, but some people subscribe to them extrinsically for purely practical, social, or self-serving reasons, that is because they pay off in the long run. Others may adopt and adhere to them intrinsically with great passion either for their own sake, as a matter of principle, because they are rewarded, or for the common good, and with great intensity of feeling and commitment. There is no definitive list of carefully considered conscience-sanctioned ethical rules, but they include such things as:

We ought to keep our promises.

We ought to tell the truth.

We ought not to kill.

An Axiological Process Ethics

We ought not to steal.

We ought to avoid harming others.

We ought to educate our children.

We ought to relieve suffering and not inflict it.

We ought to do unto others as we would have them do unto us.

We ought to help the poor, those in need, and the least advantaged members of society.

The moral rules by which people actually try to live are always relative to and applied within particular historical conditions and circumstances. Many socially accepted and practiced moral rules are much more concrete than these, and they can be much more controversial and less obvious and appealing, for example:

We ought to provide health care for everyone (the right to health care).

We ought not to provide health care for everyone.

Abortions should be available under some circumstances.

Abortions should never be available under any circumstances.

Drinking alcohol is morally permissible.

Drinking alcohol is morally wrong.

Smoking marijuana is morally permissible.

Smoking marijuana is morally wrong.

Loving and faithful homosexual relations and commitments are morally acceptable.

All homosexual relations are morally wrong.

As widely acknowledged today, almost all moral rules require appropriate qualifications and exceptions, for example, allowing killing in self-defense, or to protect friends or loved ones against aggression when there is no other way to do it, or when required by catastrophic end of life circumstances, or to prevent far greater harms or evils. Some would add: when capital punishment is called for. Having "Thou shalt not kill" in mind, Whitehead said, "The Ten Commandments tell us that in the vast majority of cases such slaughter is better avoided. In these exceptional circumstances we avoid the term *murder*" (*MT* 14). In other words, sometimes killing isn't murder. Theologians and translators tell us that "kill" in this commandment really means "murder." Thus, it does not forbid killing "in exceptional circumstances." Whitehead himself was not very specific about this, but all absolutistic moral rules have legitimate exceptions. Kant was wrong in not allowing any exceptions to the moral maxims sanctioned by his categorical imperative, one version of which was, "Act on that maxim that you would will to become a universal law," or "a universal law of nature." Kant did not realize that we can in good conscience will that some exceptions to moral requirements and prohibitions be universally accepted and practiced!

Whitehead was very sensitive to the way in which "the details" of entrenched moral codes "are relative to the circumstances of the immediate environment" (*AI* 290). As he explained,

> Moral codes have suffered from the exaggerated claims made for them. The dogmatic fallacy has here done its worst. Each such code has been put out by a God on a mountain top, or by a Saint in a cave, or by a divine Despot on a throne, or, at the lowest, by ancestors with a wisdom beyond later question. In any case, each code is incapable of improvement; and unfortunately in details they fail to agree with each other or with our existing moral intuitions. (*AI* 290)

Still, some ethical guidelines are highly desirable, indeed practically indispensible, and are in accord with our most reflectively refined and carefully considered moral intuitions. No society could long survive where "Thou shalt murder" and "Thou shalt steal" were universally adopted and practiced. When most conscientious people (except for Kant) consult their carefully considered moral intuitions (reflectively or rationally refined conscience), they find that moral rules and laws exist for the sake of practice, property, and people, not the other way around. Laws as such are not unique, conscious, self-significant, self or other valuing, actual entities; thus they have no "sake." They exist only for our sake, for our benefit.

Can we discover a few very general and basic moral principles to use in sorting through the details of ingrained moral codes and refining or weeding out unacceptable and outmoded maxims, rules, and social practices? *Whitehead's own most general moral principle was, "Morality consists in the control of process so as to maximize importance"* (*MT* 13-14). "Importance" was his most general axiological word for "goodness." His was definitely a teleological ethics that aims at maximizing goodness, not a deontological ethics that aims at duty for its own sake. Process ethics is for the sake of people, animals, and other living or experiencing beings. Whitehead well understood that some moral codes, or aspects thereof, are more essential than others in achieving this teleological objective. In another discussion, he identified two fundamental moral principles.

> These are the principles of the generality of harmony, and of the importance of the individual. The first means 'order', and the second means 'love.' Between the two there is a suggestion of opposition. For 'order' is impersonal; and love above all things, is personal. The antithesis is solved by rating types of order in relative importance according to their success in magnifying the

individualities, that is to say, in promoting strength of experience. (*AI* 292)

Chapter Two explored difficulties with and ambiguities in Whitehead's concept of an "individual." In the above quote, did he have in mind enduring souls, particular actual occasions, or particular experiences? The answer is not clear. Anyhow, love takes priority over order, the personal over the impersonal, the intrinsic over the systemic. That is very much in harmony with axiological ethics. Order is something that we value. Love is a way of valuing intrinsically. It is how we ought to value intrinsically—where "ought" means "This would be best, so do it." Order is an object of value that may be loved for its own sake or for our sake. Which is best?

Elsewhere I summarized the most basic systemic moral principles of formal axiology in these words:

1) We ought to value people more than things, and things more than ideas.

2) We ought to develop ourselves, and to help others develop themselves, systemically, extrinsically, and intrinsically.

3) We ought to value all persons and conscious beings, including ourselves, intrinsically, and never merely extrinsically or merely systemically.

4) In all possible value dimensions, we ought to choose courses of action that sustain or increase value, and avoid actions that decrease value for ourselves and others who are affected by what we do.

5) Thus, we ought always to identify with, prefer, choose, and do what is best, that is, what is likely to be richest in good-making properties. (Edwards 2010, 170)

Systemic moral virtues are intellectual virtues applied morally, that is, in order to advance, preserve, and defend the common good. Of course, not everyone thinks that morality has the common good as its primary objective, but this is how morality is here understood. Kant thought that morality deals only with respect for the moral law for its own sake. The intellectual virtues may be applied outside of morality, or amorally, for example, to the pursuit of truth or knowledge, whether scientific, philosophical, theological, moral, or whatever. But intellectual virtues can also be applied ethically. They can be used to advance all forms of human knowledge, including moral and spiritual knowledge for the sake of general human well being, not just knowledge for its own sake. Whitehead recognized a "moral temper required for the pursuit of truth" (*SMW* 187).

There are many intellectual virtues, one of which is the defining characteristic of systemic valuation itself—*objectivity, impartiality, or fair-mindedness* when dealing with beliefs and theories. This intellectual virtue is closely allied with and spills over psychologically into the moral virtue of justice, which treats people and animals rather than ideas fairly and impartially. Another intellectual virtue is *love of truth or wisdom*—the root idea of philosophy itself—though not all truth is philosophical in nature. Some truth is common sense, some scientific, some theological, some axiological, and so on. We usually have true propositions in mind when we consider the love of truth, but Whitehead had more than propositions in mind. In his correspondence theory of truth, both propositions and appearances can correspond with realities, or fail to do so. True propositions accurately describe the situation or "nexus" to which they refer: "A proposition is true when the nexus does in reality exemplify the pattern which is the predicate of the proposition" (*AI* 244). Both appearances and propositions can be true to the degree that they reflect and share the objective property to which they correspond. Truth is "the conformity of Appearance to Reality" (265). *Intellectual honesty* that is not undermined by narrowness, prejudice, dogmatism, and self-deception is a necessary condition of truth-seeking.

How did Whitehead *evaluate truth*? He proclaimed, "It is more important that a proposition be interesting than that it be true." He quickly added, "But of course a true proposition is more apt to be interesting than a false one" (244). According to Cobb, Whitehead seems to "assign it an intrinsic value" (1965, 108), but that would be an axiological mistake. Truth is an abstraction having no subjectivity of its own. It is good for us, but not for itself.

Another intellectual virtue is *curiosity*, and we can be curious about many things, including moral issues and predicaments. With Aristotle, Whitehead recognized that all human knowledge begins with wonder, but when this has run its course and "philosophic thought has done its best, the wonder remains. There have been added, however, some grasp of the immensity of things, some purification of emotion by understanding" (*MT* 168-69). Whitehead recommended that we sit lightly and not dogmatically upon our truth claims, whether, scientific, philosophical, theological, or what have you (*PR* 8). Thus, wonder goes hand in hand with *intellectual modesty or humility*, and this intellectual virtue has great moral significance. If we had it, much of the dogmatism and intolerance present in our social order would simply disappear. Whitehead repeatedly commended this virtue and repudiated its opposite, "the dogmatic fallacy, which is the belief that the principles of its working hypothesis are clear, obvious, and irreformable" (*AI* 223). His own fallibilistic view was, "Philosophers can never hope finally to formulate these metaphysical first principles. Weakness of insight and deficiencies of language stand in the way inexorably" (*PR* 4), and "Rationalism is an adventure in the clarification of thought, progressive and never final. But it is an adventure in which even partial success has importance" (9; see also 13, 20, 193).

Of course, we all need intellectual humility, not just philosophers. Robert S. Hartman also expressed intellectual humility and fallibilism when he indicated, "The axiom of value is *objective*. It is valid for every rational being whatever. . . . But its application is *subjective*" (1967, 110), and "Oddly enough, my own philosophy has taught me the relative unimportance of my philosophy" (1994, 94). Here Hartman was comparing the importance of philosophy with that of intrinsically valuable unique persons. People come first, even before philosophy.

EXTRINSIC ETHICS AND EXTRINSIC VIRTUES

Extrinsic ethics is a personally or socially useful ethics, and it is adopted precisely because it is personally or socially useful. As personally useful, it consists in *acting* in ways that ordinarily work toward a worthwhile life and one's own good, and in being adequately informed, motivated, and disposed so to do. As socially useful, it consists in *acting* rightly in ways that ordinarily work toward worthwhile lives for everyone, for the common good, and in being adequately informed, motivated, and disposed so to do. Often, as in long-range egoism, the two rationales and motivations are conflated because up to some point it is personally beneficial to promote the well-being of others.

The primary focus of extrinsic ethics is on actions and their consequences. Extrinsic ethics includes and presupposes systemic ethics. Acting without information is blind, foolish, and morally perverse. Despite what Kant said about it, knowing the likely consequences of our actions is highly relevant to what we ought to do. Becoming adequately informed is a moral imperative. Moral ignorance is immoral.

Rationally, extrinsic ethics involves understanding then acting knowingly in accord with personally and socially beneficial moral rules, recognizing that good moral judgment often transcends rule-rigidity. It considers actions, their maxims, their motives, and their consequences, unlike Kant's formal systemic ethics, which officially ignored desires, feelings, and consequences. It requires being informed about what is likely to help or hurt people, thinking helpful rather than hurtful thoughts, bringing other-regarding moral desires and feelings to bear, and putting systemic value insights into practice. It thinks positive or beneficial rather than negative, hurtful, degrading, or prejudicial thoughts about people because harmful thoughts often lead to harmful deeds and to real harm to persons.

Utilitarian ethical theories focus primarily on extrinsic practical concerns, on personal and common good, and so do most process ethicists, though they do not neglect information, moral rules, and moral motives. Recall the discussion of Hartshorne's view of ethics at the end of Chapter Three. Affectively, extrinsic moral goodness involves very ordinary everyday human feelings, emotions, pleasures, attitudes, preferences, approvals, attitudes, likings, desires, and interests. Practically, it involves *acting* prudently or rightly, which goes deeper than just being rationally objective and informed about relevant rules and facts.

Extrinsic moral virtues are widely accepted and socially enforced moral practices, not just moral theories. They are for the sake of people, not the moral law. Pro-social beliefs, feelings, and desires, if often enough taught, practiced, and reinforced, can become moral habits, dispositions, and virtues. Virtues are not single good-doing deeds, as Aristotle well understood. We are virtuous only when doing good to self and others is so deeply ingrained in our personalities that it becomes almost second nature to us and dispositional within us. Practice is what creates such deeply embedded habits of soul.

Extrinsically virtuous people are very practical, and they typically follow socially beneficial moral guidelines and develop moral virtues, practices, and habits—mainly because they expect morality to pay off to themselves in the long run. "Honesty pays," and "Every good deed will be rewarded." Extrinsic ethics is mainly just long-range egoism or selfishness, and it presupposes the metaphysical reality of isolated non-relational souls that simply do not exist. What philosophers call "reciprocal altruism" is a good expression of extrinsic moral goodness. The social contract is only a "fiction," as Whitehead recognized (*AI* 56), but most people, for very practical reasons, find it very appealing, at least half-consciously, because it codifies and formalizes long-range self-interests, and to some degree it connects self-interest with other-regards. "I won't hurt you if you won't hurt me; I will help you if you will help me." "I will scratch your back if you will scratch mine." "You need me now, but I will need you later." Thereby we get along and muddle through.

If accepted only for their usefulness to ourselves, the effective scope of my (or anyone's) extrinsic social-contract ethical codes and practices is limited to those who will most likely favor me if I favor them. Though not easily and consciously recognized, in its purest form, an extrinsically ethical life grounded on reciprocal altruism involves constant score-keeping and bartering with others. Only those likely to repay have moral standing, receive favors, and deserve respect. Having moral standing means being recognized as someone to whom moral duties are owed. Outsiders and relatively powerless and low status inferiors don't count. Low probabilities of payback are discounted. So the rich and powerful become richer and more powerful, aided by others who are also rich and powerful, and the "least of these" are ignored, degraded, and exploited. This is the way of the world. To one degree or another members of every social group or class take care of one another, usually for extrinsic reasons of long-range self-interest, but at times from more profound intrinsic moral virtues. Basically selfish people occasionally have genuinely unselfish thoughts, feelings, desires, and deeds. Also, the line between insiders and outsiders is always fuzzy and arbitrary, but most people live by the distinction much of the time. Fortunately, in most people extrinsic social contract ethics is seldom pure.

The most influential social contract theorist of our time, John Rawls, assumed that the fictional individuals making an original social contract would be completely egoistic or self-interested and have no trace of unselfishness in their souls. Since we are by nature social beings, most real people are not such complete egoists. We are motivated at times to help a few others in genuinely unselfish ways, so the line between extrinsic and intrinsic morality grows fuzzy in application and practice, depending on the depth and scope of other-regarding beliefs, imperatives, desires, affections, practices, and behaviors. Most ordinary people are at least systemically or extrinsically ethical or virtuous much of the time and get along well enough with others without being moral saints and heroes. Most people follow the rules, or at least some of them, as a matter of social pressure, habit, conformity, and self-interest. They are convinced that doing so will pay off to themselves in the long run. By degrees, and from habit, social pressure, and reciprocal altruism, they exemplify such moral virtues as truthfulness, promise-keeping, generosity, kindness, courage, temperance, justice, humility, honesty, forgiveness, and many others.

Extrinsic practical ethics makes only minimal moral demands on ordinary people. It requires no more than the most socially useful minimal moral virtues. It does not require ordinary people to be saints and heroes at all times. It does not require what philosophers call "supererogation," or "going beyond the call of duty." Its moral rules and virtues are so essential for successful communal living that psychological, social, or legal penalties are associated with disobeying them, as John Stuart Mill recognized. Mill is often misinterpreted, but he was only a minimizing

Utilitarian, not a maximizer claiming that we are always morally obligated to do what is best, to maximize goodness (Edwards, 1986, 1999). Whitehead, by contrast, was a maximizer. Mill thought that only the most basic, but not the most demanding, moral rules and ideals should be socially enforced with penalties for violations. These penalties ("sanctions," Mill called them) range from a guilty conscience, to various manifestations of public social disapproval, to legal penalties of varying degrees, proportional ideally to the harm done by lawbreakers and offenders.

Extrinsic moral virtue involves very little, if anything, that transcends long-range self-interest. It acknowledges that my good and the common good are deeply intertwined. As an ethic for ordinary people, not for saints and heroes, extrinsic morality does not require acting to *maximize* goodness or importance at all times. It does not moralize the whole of life, as does intrinsic ethics. It does not insist upon maximum ethical development, expression, motives, feelings, temperaments, or virtues. Ordinary and extraordinary thoughts, motives, behaviors, and traits of character gradually shade off into one another, but extrinsic practical ethics stops short of the highest moral virtues of constant and genuinely unselfish universal love, compassion, and self-sacrifice (if need be). These are required only in optimal intrinsic virtue ethics.

Protecting fundamental *human rights* falls within the realm of everyday extrinsic ethics. Rights identify and affirm the most socially and personally beneficial and indispensable moral rules of all. They forbid doing things to people (and animals?) that violate the most critical inner core of anyone's subjectivity, uniqueness, and intrinsic worth, including our own, or else they require that things be done (e.g., providing public education or universal health care) that are essential for preserving, developing, and expressing that inner core of worth (Edwards 2010, 145-47). Rights are so indispensable for preserving morally decent and livable societies that the most severe social and legal penalties and sanctions ought to be and usually are attached to rights offenses and violations. Sadly, immoral or barely moral societies are not so arranged. Social orders that do no recognize and protect human rights are miserable places to live. In such societies, immorality is deeply entrenched, and life is "solitary, nasty, poor, brutish, and short" (Hobbes).

There is no "official" list of fundamental moral rights, but we are familiar with the rights to "life, liberty, and the pursuit of happiness." The Bill of Rights to the U.S. Constitution identifies many more. Additional examples are carefully examined and defended in John Cobb's *Matters of Life and Death*. There, whole chapters are devoted to the rights to kill, to die, to live, and to love. Like other moral rules, rights-rules may conflict with each other, and there are legitimate exceptions. Rights claims can be overdone, as when anything that anybody wants is said to be their right. They can also be overridden by stronger rights claims. My rights to life and self-defense override your right to life if you are trying to kill me. My right to property overrides your right to liberty if you have stolen something substantial from me; you may land in jail. The pregnant woman's rights to life and self-defense override that of the fetus when her life is at stake—admittedly a more controversial example.

Rights claims are often controversial, and many rights have to be won the hard way, then defended constantly and vigorously. Slaves in earlier America understood this perfectly well, as have their segregated and discriminated-against descendants. Until 1920, women had no right to vote in this country. There is still no equal pay for equal work. Minorities, women, and persons with diverse sexual preferences are still struggling for their rights. Immoral societies can be improved and moved toward respecting rights, and moral societies can decline and fall. Which way are we going?

Whitehead acknowledged the historicity and vulnerability of human rights: "The growth of the idea of the essential rights of human beings, arising from their sheer humanity, affords a striking example of the history of ideas." Then he proceeded directly to a discussion of slavery (*AI* 14). Rights really don't arise from "sheer humanity." They arise from our five defining properties of intrinsic goodness, shared by degrees with non-human animals. If relevant, by degrees many non-human animals are rational animals and are plenty capable of outsmarting us at times.

One person's rights correlate with the moral duties of others. There are no rights without duties. If you have a right to freedom, others have a duty not to enslave you, or to liberate you, or to mitigate your burdens. If you have a right to freedom of speech, others have a duty to allow you to express yourself and be heard. If you have a right to a basic education and to basic health care, society has (taxpayers have), a duty to provide them. If you have a right to freedom of religion, others are obligated to leave you alone, even if they disagree with you. Everyone is duty-bound not to use the powers of the state, or any other powers or principalities, to force you to adopt a religious outlook that you cannot in good conscience accept.

INTRINSIC ETHICS AND INTRINSIC VIRTUES

Intrinsic ethics is more challenging than systemic and extrinsic ethics, and intrinsic virtues are more intense, diverse, comprehensive, developed, constant, and demanding. Intrinsic ethics includes but goes beyond both systemic and extrinsic ethics. Rationally, it applies the Form of the Good, the common good, maximally to self and all others. Affectively, it is the most intense and comprehensive ethics of all.

Intrinsically virtuous people consider and are guided by moral rules (rational or systemic ethics), but they recognize that rules are incomplete, general, and often conflicting. Rules and principles can never compensate for or take the place of good judgment by good people in concrete circumstances. The most fundamental principle of intrinsic ethics is: "We ought always to identify with, prefer, choose, and do what is best, that is, what is likely to be richest in good-making properties" (Edwards 2010, 156). Applying this leaves considerable room for individual judgment, especially in very common situations where moral guidelines are in conflict or are not clear. There is a very close link between virtues and right acts in intrinsic ethics. Love, empathy, and compassion are among the principal virtues of intrinsic ethics, so intrinsic ethics is an intrinsic virtue ethics. *The right or most ethical act is always the one that informed, fair, loving, empathetic, and compassionate people would do.* For this, there are no precise and detailed moral rules. "Love," said Whitehead, is "a little oblivious as to morals" (*PR* 343).

Whitehead probably did not realize that he was calling for *optimal virtue*, but his own "Morality consists in the control of process so as to maximize importance" (*MT* 13-14) expresses what philosophers call an optimal or maximizing ethics, an intrinsic ethics of saintly and heroic actions and virtues, an ethics of acting always to maximize goodness both socially and personally, an ethics that goes beyond minimal decency and reciprocal altruism. Whitehead clearly thought that ethics subjectively aims at *maximizing goodness or importance*. Even so, that is only a matter of degree in practice. Intrinsically virtuous people are both informed and active, so intrinsic virtue ethics includes extrinsic ethics as well as systemic ethics. Intrinsic ethics requires more than conforming to a socially enforceable minimum of moral decency, though intrinsically virtuous people do that, and more. John Stuart Mill was right: A maximizing ethics should *not* be socially *enforced;* there should be no penalties for not being saints and heroes at all times. Optimal goodness is desirable but not obligatory. Maximal goodness can and should be *encouraged* in an immense variety of ways, just as Mill said (Edwards 1986, 1999), but we are not duty-bound with penalties for failure to be saints and heroes all the time. Our present worldly and self-centered social order, as well as our entertainment and social media, largely promote wickedness and fail to encourage goodness.

Intrinsic virtues subjectively aim at and move toward saintliness, maximal moral goodness, and what is best for everyone, including animals and all living things. Intrinsic virtues aim to maximize importance, not just to satisfy some socially enforceable minimum. They go beyond the minimal and enforceable call of duty. Affectively, intrinsic virtues include profound manifestations of morally good or socially beneficial motives and enduring ethical affections and traits of character. As I wrote elsewhere,

> With increasing degrees of intensity and specification, all three levels of morality orient us toward and are governed by the basic principle of morality: We ought always to identify, prefer, choose, and do what is best, that is, what is likely to be richest in good-making properties. The systemic level gives more specific action-guiding moral rules for optimizing moral goodness; the extrinsic level largely lives it but without great passion; the intrinsic level does it best, most thoroughly, and with the most intense, profound, and saintly moral motives and virtues. (Edwards 2010, 156)

Anything can be valued in any value dimension, as previously explained. So, if true to form, systemically virtuous people are objectively or dispassionately moral, and they are guided by reflectively refined moral rules just because they are there. Extrinsically ethical people are practically and minimally moral, and they work for the common good as long as that is likely to pay off to themselves in the long run. Intrinsically ethical people are maximally moral, and their virtues exceed those of reciprocal altruism. They are genuinely unselfish, loving, empathetic, compassionate, and just. They manifest all common and extraordinary virtues at their best, especially those discussed below.

Morally good people can be systemically, extrinsically, or intrinsically virtuous by degrees. Well-known and widely practiced extrinsic-level moral virtues are wisdom, courage, generosity, kindness, temperance, justice, humility, truthfulness, honesty, forgiveness, etc. Other moral virtues like love, empathy, and compassion, and profound justice involve distinctively intrinsic and less commonplace modes of evaluation that transcend long range self-interests. When mature these manifest the most intense and profound intrinsic evaluations of others and self. Since the three dimensions of ethics shade into one another, ordinary people who are less than saints and heroes often manifest degrees of love, empathy, compassion, and justice. Yet, their loves, sympathies, and equities are usually limited to "kin and kind," as sociobiologists would say. By comparison, the intrinsic virtues of saints and heroes tend toward both intensity and universality. So what are *some* of their virtues?

Refined conscience. All people, by nature, and not just by culture, have an internal moral compass, commonly called "conscience." Even systemically and extrinsically virtuous people have a working conscience, even if grounded mainly in self-interest. The clarity and strength of conscience vary from person to person. Conscience and its mandates may be colored or distorted by culture, upbringing, social pressures, and temptations; but we all have one (except maybe sociopaths).

The moral intuitions of intrinsically virtuous people have been carefully considered and reflectively refined. Conscience approves of certain ways of relating to people for the common good and disapproves of others. It comes in three dimensions and three levels of refinement. Some people are stuck on principles and formalities. Most morally decent people are attuned to systemic and extrinsic practicalities because they pay. Morally advanced people are attuned to and live in accord with a more reflectively refined, objective, and affectively mature intrinsic conscience. They have an easy conscience because they actually do what a mature three dimensional conscience requires, and they refrain from what reflectively refined conscience forbids. No one can be a morally good person systemically, extrinsically, or intrinsically without conscience, an intuitive sense of and beliefs about moral good and evil, right and wrong, and actions flowing from them. Being intensely conscientious—thinking, feeling, and acting conscientiously—will enrich our lives, even though self-enrichment is not their intended or intentional object.

Empathy. Intrinsic empathy goes further than conscience alone, which could not function effectively without some degree of empathy. Empathy is the ability to imagine oneself in someone else's place, in "someone else's shoes," as we often say. Empathy feels and positively values the goodness in someone else's life, whether it be systemic (mental), extrinsic (physical, material, social, active, or practical), or intrinsic (inner, personal, unique). Empathy requires *imagination, information, and feeling*. It functions when we understand, imagine, feel, and affirm the goodness (or badness) in someone's else's life, especially in those circumstances where our own thoughts, feelings, words, and actions might impact their well or ill being. Imagining and valuing what is going on inside others, how we might affect them for better or for worse, and how they would likely respond to our influence, forms and informs the highest or best ethical behavior.

One of the most important and universally accepted formal aids to empathy is commonly called the Golden Rule. Exactly what it says may be expressed in many different ways: Do unto others as you would have them do unto you. Do not do unto others what you would not have them do unto you. Do not hurt others if you would not have them hurt you.

Desire for others what you would desire for yourself. Love for others what you would love for yourself. Love others as you love yourself. All versions of the Golden Rule require vividly imagining how others would be affected by what we do, *assuming that we have their thoughts, beliefs, feelings, desires, habits, and interests,* not that they have ours. Intrinsically virtuous persons are profoundly empathetic and act accordingly. Empathy is a fundamental good-making-property of morally mature and saintly persons. Being empathetic also enriches our own lives, even though self-enrichment is not its intended object.

Compassion. Empathy focuses on positive *goodness* in the lives of others, and on acting to enhance that goodness. Compassion attends to *undesirable things or harms* in the lives of others, and on acting to alleviate or avoid them. Empathy rejoices with those who rejoice; compassion suffers with those who suffer. Some evils in the lives of others are systemic (undesirable thoughts and beliefs, falsehoods, confusions, ignorance, contradictions). Some evils are extrinsic (undesirable physical or social conditions or behaviors), or intrinsic (undesirable inner or personal conditions, experiences, activities, feelings, desires, interests, conflicts, or suffering). Evils in the lives of others are not necessarily inflicted by us. They may be already there, imposed by existing social or natural causes, or by what they have done in the past. Compassionate people identify profoundly with the sufferings and losses of others. They also do what they can to console those who suffer and to prevent or alleviate their sufferings and losses. Compassion imagines and feels the harms that we might inflict on others, or that they otherwise suffer, and it is merciful. Compassion does not inflict harms on others that we would not wish to have inflicted on ourselves, and it acts to alleviate already existing harms and distresses that we would want relieved if we were in their place. Being compassionate also enriches our own lives, even though self-enrichment is not its intended object.

Identification with and love for others. Empathy and compassion manifest an underlying intense axiological/psychological love for and identification with others. Artistic, practical, and intellectual creativity, concentration and consumption involve intense personal identification with works of art, physical things, social conditions in the world, and intellectual products. We may robustly identify ourselves with systemic goods, with extrinsic goods, and with intrinsic goods. *Love* is our most common word for profound intrinsic identification. We can love things, thoughts, and unique conscious beings. Our loves should be ordered according to the hierarchy of value.

When we identify ourselves profoundly and lovingly with intrinsically valuable people, animals, etc., something very strange and interesting happens to us. We are transformed. We are no longer narrowly and exclusively self-interested or self-centered. The "self" is changed into something much more inclusive and expansive. The self-fulfillment derived from identifying with others is no longer selfish, for we are no longer exclusively self-interested selves. As Whitehead recognized, "Morality of outlook is inseparably conjoined with generality of outlook. The antithesis between the general good and the individual interest can be abolished only when the individual is such that its interest is the general good" (*PR* 15).

Psychologically and axiologically, we somehow become one with others in love, compassion, and all identification experiences. Their interests become our own interests. Ontologically, we are still unique and distinct individuals, but our total internal self-identity now includes their self-identity, or what we can make of it. The metaphysical differences between us no longer matter and may no longer even be noticed. Their systemic, extrinsic, and intrinsic goodness become our systemic, extrinsic, and intrinsic goodness. The systemic, extrinsic, and intrinsic harms that befall them now befall us psychologically and axiologically. Their well or ill being become our own well or ill being. When we love and identify intensely with others, our lives are enriched immensely but not selfishly. Their good-making properties in every value dimension become our own good-making properties. We become new, transformed, and ethically "born again" selves. We are no longer the narrowly self-absorbed persons we were before. Even with respect to their ills, our lives are enriched as we suffer compassionately with those who suffer and strive earnestly to help them and know them better. Identifying with and loving others enriches our lives, even though self-enrichment is not intended.

Intrinsic integrity. Being consistently or constantly true to ourselves, to the goodness that is in us, to the best that is in us, to our highest ethical and spiritual intuitions and ideals, is integrity. Morally good persons have systemic integrity, extrinsic integrity, and intrinsic integrity. Intrinsic integrity is its highest degree and includes all the others. By degrees, morally good people are well-informed, honest, truthful, responsible, reliable, and conscientious, loving, and compassionate. They have high standards. They are intellectually honest and avoid dogmatism and self-deception. They are dependably helpful and actually live up to their highest ideals of goodness, again by degrees. They are open to finding and becoming something even better. They assume personal responsibility for who and what they are, think, believe, feel, and do. They have profound self-esteem and value themselves as well as others intrinsically. Having integrity enriches us, though self-enrichment is not its intended object.

Many other moral virtues could be identified and discussed, e.g., *a sense of justice* that issues in treating people fairly and with due respect, but perhaps enough has been said about the special intrinsic moral virtues that should be emphasized by an axiological process virtue ethics. *Morally right actions* are those that would be done by people with integrity who are informed, conscientious, empathetic, compassionate, and loving, who identify themselves with others, who are consistently true or faithful in thoughts, words, desires, and deeds to the best of the goodness within themselves, and who are fair and just in their dealings with others. Moral rules are never sufficiently precise or inclusive to eliminate the necessity for the individual judgments and decisions of virtuous people.

Many hard questions about how to apply an axiological process ethics doubtless remain to be answered, but preceding discussions indicate what it might imply for a few highly controversial issues in medical ethics, ethics and animals, ethics and the environment, conflicts between intrinsically valuable lives, degrees of intrinsic goodness, abortions, killing people and animals, etc. Many very satisfactory applications of process morality to ethical particularities are now readily available elsewhere (Cobb 1991 and 2003; Henning 2005). The present book aims primarily at developing and expanding the theoretical horizons of process ethics into a more adequate axiological process ethics.

Without attempting to cover the very large topic of moral vices and negative thoughts, deeds, and feelings, consider next a few common but serious obstacles to becoming and being morally virtuous persons. Familiar vices like hatred, malice, selfishness, and greed definitely have a place in what follows.

MAJOR OBSTACLES TO VIRTUOUS LIVING

Not everyone is morally good. Bad people exist in the world, and most people occupy a fuzzy realm somewhere between the best and the worst that they could be. Bad people are intrinsically good but morally bad, again by degrees. Why is it so hard for us to be or become morally good people? Here are a few of the many obstacles. Their causes are manifold.

Undervaluing other people and animals is quite commonplace. Even when we attach some positive value to people and animals, as most of us usually do, we may regard them as having less value than they actually have, and we may think, feel, and act accordingly. We may value them only or primarily extrinsically. This happens when we exploit them and treat them as mere means to our own ends, fail to acknowledge their intrinsic worth, do not take adequate account of their own beliefs, plans, projects, physical well being, or inner feelings, desires, preferences, habits, and interests, and do not treat them as ends in themselves.

It *is* morally permissible to use people and animals; we do it appropriately and with proper respect much of the time; but we may not *merely* use people or animals and disregard or disvalue their inner reality, feelings, interests, preferences, and intrinsic worth. We may overvalue the extrinsic and undervalue the intrinsic. We often disregard or thwart what is best for others for the sake of our own material or social gains, thus undervaluing their intrinsic goodness for the sake of our own extrinsic well being. We may undervalue and put down others who disagree with us, or those who do not fit neatly into our own belief systems and ways of thinking, thus ranking their intrinsic personal worth lower than our own systemic conceptual values. Ideologists, fanatics, authoritarians, dogmatists, and tyrants of every description consistently do this, or worse.

Not valuing others intrinsically actually diminishes us, though we may not realize it. We hurt ourselves when we do not identify with others, with human and non-human animals, with all good things. We include less goodness than we could when we do not take their complete goodness into ourselves and make it our own, unselfishly. People can be very moral in some ways, e.g., systemically and extrinsically, without being profoundly or intrinsically moral, that is, without being very loving and compassionate toward all, without identifying with all goodness in all. People who know what is right and act accordingly may be extrinsically moral (because it pays), or systemically moral [duty only for the sake of duty, or only "for the sake of the law" (Kant 6-7, 18-20)]—but not for the sake of people, animals, and all unique subjects. Yet, such people are missing out on something very important.

Egoists, enviers, and reciprocal altruists are selfish. They may actually resent the fact that innumerable good things belong to and within others. They may regret that all the goodness in the universe is not exclusively their own. Yet, anyone can make all the goodness in the universe their own by not caring that it is not exclusively their own, by delighting in and being grateful for its presence with and in others, and by identifying as fully as possible with the goodness of all in all. That is how God values the world. The lives of such intrinsically moral (and saintly) people are as meaningful and abundant in goodness as it is possible for any human life to be.

Disvaluing other people and animals goes beyond the practical error of axiological undervaluation. We may regard people as having little or no value, as worthless, but we may go even further and regard them (and even animals) as so inherently evil that we are allowed if not obligated to inflict evils of any or every description upon them by any means available to us. We may regard others, our "enemies," as inherently evil because they now threaten, or in the past have damaged, our way of thinking, our social prestige or material prosperity, or our inner feelings and reality. Of course, they may have the same view of us!

Moral vices like hatred, malice, and revenge disvalue people as such, and they are miserable states of mind. People fuming with prejudice, hatred, malice, and revenge do not realize how miserable they make themselves! Greed and envy disvalue ownership by others while positively coveting their good stuff for ourselves. Dogmatism, intolerance, and ideology disvalue their beliefs and life-forms if different from our own. These vices are major obstacles to both moral goodness and worthwhile living.

Better means richer in goodness, or poorer in badness. Love is better than hatred and malice. Forgiveness and mercy are better than revenge. Delight in the prosperity of others is better than greed and envy. Equality is better than snobbery or domineering. Inclusion is better than exclusion. Tolerance is better than dogmatism. Helping is better than hurting. Building is better than destroying. Peace is better than war. Apparently, these are difficult moral lessons for anyone anywhere to learn and practice, but the world would be a much better place for all if we did.

The insider/outsider distinction is perfectly natural but morally pernicious. Sometimes, the right thing to do is *not to follow nature!* Almost everyone (except for moral saints) lives by this distinction. Insiders are people who have moral standing with us; they belong to our moral community; outsiders don't. We have moral duties to them, but not to outsiders. For most people, non-human animals are outsiders. "Low down" people in our own social order have lesser social rank and standing and are barely inside our moral circle, if they count at all. We sense that we have moral duties to help and not hurt insiders, but not outsiders. Insiders are "our kind of people;" outsiders are "those kind of people," useless people, inferiors, dissenters, strangers, oddballs, aliens, outcasts, enemies. By degrees we care about what happens to insiders, but not to outsiders and inferiors, not to people who are different. Through the insider/outsider distinction we inordinately limit the scope of our moral concerns, feelings, duties, and frames of reference. We regularly employ it to ignore, underestimate, or even disvalue the intrinsic worth of others, both non-human and human animals. We express our adherence to it in an immense variety of ways—class consciousness, snobbery, cliquishness, bullying, bigotry, arrogance, rudeness, incivility, domineering, authoritarianism, racism, sexism, homophobia, nationalism, partisanship, profiling, religious exclusivism, and prejudice of every description.

We spend millions of dollars every year buying guns and ammunition to protect ourselves from outsiders in our midst. Even very good people will not be pushed very far away from favoring insiders in many many ways. Few if any of us are perfect.

Modern sociobiologists, beginning with Darwin, tell us that when morality first originated, it was applied only to members of one's own tribe or clan, but not to outsiders, not to those who did not belong. By nature, we seem to care morally only for kin and kind. Extrinsic ethics is natural; intrinsic ethics is sublime and divine. Even within our own social groups and cultures, we distinguish between superiors and inferiors, and we think that we have less stringent moral obligations to inferiors, perhaps none at all. Many philosophers, theologians, and others insist that we must somehow expand the scope of our moral concerns beyond kin, kind, social class, nationality, and species. Philosophers (who often do not know what "the real world" is like) insist that *by definition* morality is necessarily universal in scope and application. If only definitions could make it so! Many others, especially religious thinkers, say that we are all brothers, sisters, and equal children of God, and we should think, feel, and act accordingly. Are they fighting a losing battle with human nature? Let us hope not.

ETHICAL AND SPIRITUAL VALUES AND EVALUATIONS

In due time, ethical self-realization and integrity almost inevitably spill over into spiritual self-realization and integrity. Not necessarily so, but this depends largely on what we mean by "ethics," now defined, and "spirituality," not yet defined. Many "unchurched" people say, especially to pollsters, that they are very "spiritual" but not "religious." By "religious" they mean "organized religion." In other words, they are spiritual, but they don't go to church, or synagogue, or mosque, or whatever. Church membership and attendance have drastically declined, very noticeably since around 1990, yet many people still claim to be spiritual. So what do they mean by "spiritual"? Many different things, so it seems.

They may mean that they are *systemically religious,* that is, that they still somehow accept, positively value, or at least search for religious beliefs like God, Jesus, heaven and hell, or something ultimate, immaterial, positive, optimistic, or sacred that makes life meaningful.

Sometimes they just mean *extrinsically ethical.* They mean that they are morally decent and tolerant people (mainly at systemic/extrinsic levels) despite the fact that they don't go to church, synagogue, mosque, or whatever. They feel morally connected in some way to others and try to live accordingly. They positively value social interdependence. They still recognize that we are members of one another.

They may mean that they go some place other than the church and other religious institutions to find social support and expression for their morality and spirituality, however they conceive of them. They may think that established religious institutions are hopelessly identified with obsolete issues and perspectives and look elsewhere for their religious worldviews. They find new spiritual communities on TV, the Internet, or through some other contemporary medium or electronic device.

They may mean that they have special *spiritual sensitivities and experiences* of some kind. They practice meditation, achieve inner peace, or occasionally have mystical experiences, which can vary immensely in kind and content—when they have any content at all. Some mystics cultivate spiritual experiences of emptiness, of pure consciousness with no content whatsoever, so they tell us.

They may mean something more definite, theistic, holistic, and intrinsic. They may mean that they *intrinsically experience the presence of God* in themselves, in other people, and in all of creation. This is what

I would personally mean by "spiritual." The spiritual support, wisdom, and practices of congregations really do help with this! Finding God is easier with social support than in solitude, though there is a place for both. When we find God, we find all others.

Of course, "God" can mean many different things to different people. For the sake of the discussion, let us assume that the word refers to a Supreme Reality having most if not all of the attributes assigned to God in classical and process theology. Even this obviously allows plenty of room for disagreement and for multiple interpretations, but it narrows things down a bit. The important thing is that our theological words point or refer to an objectively existing God, and that they evoke and reflect our experience or sense of God's presence. Always, there is much room for improvement in our wording and thinking about God.

"Ethical" can have many interesting and very close relations with "spiritual" in this theistic sense. We do not want to equate the two, as does the second "spiritual means ethical" option above. In many contexts, we want to say that a person can be ethical without being spiritual. But do we really want to say that a person can be spiritual without being ethical? Clearly, people who are only *minimally moral* at systemic and extrinsic levels can be ethical without being spiritual, but what about those who are *maximally ethical* in all three dimensions, especially the inclusive intrinsic? Maximally rather than minimally, "ethical" and "spiritual" may be intimately related, cover much of the same ground, have the same extension. How so? Here are a few possibilities.

First, there could be considerable overlap in scope or extensional reference in the aims of each. Ethics aims at the *common good*. We now know about "the good," but just how much is covered by "common"? Maximally, exactly who or what has moral standing or belongs to the community of our moral concerns, beliefs, duties, deeds, and feelings?

How broad is *the scope* of the community of those having moral standing and rights, of those who are entitled to societal protections and provisions, of individuals having intrinsic worth? What is the ultimate extent of the community covered by our concept of "the common good"? Once, only kin and kind were included in morality, and this is still so today in much of the so called "real world." On a typical theoretical, philosophical, moral, or spiritual level, all human beings are included, not just kin and kind. More than that, animals may be included, or at least those most like us. Even *all* animals may be granted moral standing and rights. So may plants, whole ecosystems, entire planetary systems. Real saints include all in all.

If intrinsically valuable living things exist on other planets in our Milky Way, or even in other galaxies far far away, would they be included in our understanding of "the common good"? If so, where do we stop? Given the process/axiological understanding of intrinsic goodness developed in this book, all actual entities have intrinsic worth, so there is no place to stop with respect to *valuing them for their own sakes*. Whitehead suggested something like this when he wrote, "Everything has some value for itself, for others, and for the whole" (*MT* 111). Does that mean that the whole values us, or merely that we should value the whole? Or both? If we value the whole, there is no place to stop.

Does this whole have a soul and self-significance? Is this whole God? Perhaps so. Theistic spirituality involves the sense and conviction that our values are supported by the ultimate nature of things, by the fundamental structure of the universe, by God who transcends but is yet immanent within the universe. About "the experience of deity," Whitehead wrote, "The universe is thus understood as including a source of ideals" (*AI* 103). All the ideals and aims of concresceing actual entities come from God, who is "the poet of the world, with tender patience leading it by his vision of truth, beauty, and goodness" (*PR* 346).

Intrinsically valuing all intrinsic value-objects (actual occasions, electrons, protons, extraterrestrials, people who lived long ago, and all those we cannot influence) is not the same thing as *having moral duties to them*. Ethically advanced people and spiritual saints both identify intensely with and delight in the existence of the common good, that is, with all goodness in all everywhere and every-when. The "duty" part of ethics, acting to promote the common good, covers less than the "intrinsic valuation" part, rejoicing in and identifying with the common good. Some puffs of existence are just too trivial to call for moral obligations and actions on our part, and we don't even know how to affect them. Others we just don't know enough about. Others beyond our planet in galaxies far, far away are clearly out of our reach, as are those earthlings who lived in the distant past, and those now far removed from our influence. Yet, maximally ethical people rejoice in and identify with the existence and goodness of all in all, including the systemic goodness of their truth and beliefs, the extrinsic goodness of useful and beautiful aggregates and beneficial behaviors, and the intrinsic goodness of conscious valuing subjects far, far away, those we cannot affect, those long dead and gone, yes, even the Neanderthals, dinosaurs, and trilobites. Their ethical concerns for the common good stretch into the spiritual. Their ethics is a saintly ethics. All unique, experiencing, valuing actualities, even those we cannot affect or know anything about, are both intrinsically good and sacred, partly because they have or had self-significance, but also because God is or was present in them, and they are present in God. In that, moral and spiritual saints can and do delight.

There is at least a psychological/existential link between valuing all actualities for their own sakes, even if we can't influence them, and valuing them as sacred in a theistic context, where God made them and is in them through divine influence, immanence, and omnipresence. Process theology makes good sense of God's presence in the world and beyond. According to Whitehead, "Every event on its finer side introduces God into the world.... The world lives by its incarnation of God in itself" (*RM* 155-56). Spirituality delights and rejoices in all goodness as sacred and as sub-species of eternity. This includes everything close at hand and all that is far removed from us, and it delights in and expresses gratitude for all. The "common good" extends all the way through the universe to God.

In classical theology, God acts on the world, but the world never acts on God. In process thought, we can affect God for better or worse, so we have direct ethical duties to God, or to "the whole," even if not to such trivial parts of the whole as protons and fleeting individual actual occasions, or not to far distant extraterrestrials or terrestrials who cannot be affected by what we do. Every bit of our own goodness, moral and non-moral, is ultimately contributed to God, who gives it and us objective immortality, perhaps even more. God also takes all of our sins and shortcomings and all of the tragedies of the world into and upon Godself. We should have compassion for God because God suffers every ill inflicted on everyone and everything everywhere, including those harmed by natural processes, those we harm, those harmed by others in our own little corner of the universe, and those harmed far, far away or long, long ago. In his omnipresence, God is even present in evil—passively, receptively, sensitively. This does not mean that God causes all evil; it means that all evil causes God—to suffer. There is a wideness in God's mercy that extends to all the worlds God's hands have made. God takes all the world's sins, evils, sufferings, and losses into and upon Godself. Jesus is perhaps our best historical revelation and paradigm of this. God is our fellow sufferer who understands; we can become God's fellow sufferers who understand.

A slightly different but complementary approach to blending maximal ethics with spirituality is found in identification-with-others experiences.

People who are profoundly ethical may also be profoundly spiritual without knowing it. They may have remarkable intrinsic evaluation experiences in which they lose themselves, then surprisingly discover that thereby they gain new selves, better selves, along with all goodness in all. Depending on the scope of "common," there is considerable overlap if not identity between maximal ethical concern for and identification with our common good and spiritual concern for and identification with our common God and God's own concerns. Both profoundly ethical and profoundly spiritual people identify themselves completely with all others. Thereby they take all the goodness of others into themselves and make it their own, and the more the better. This means loving and identifying with all unique subjects and all of their positive qualities, both moral and non-moral. Thereby, ethical/spiritual saints become entirely new selves, born again selves who are far more loving and value-inclusive, thereby far richer internally in their own intrinsic goodness and well-being. Thereby, they come to love and include all goodness everywhere and in everyone as their own. Thereby, unselfishness is unintentionally self-rewarding and self-fulfilling. In losing themselves in wonder, love, and grace, they find themselves. Such growth in grace is a lifelong process that never comes to an end. Love is both a spiritual and a moral virtue. As Whitehead said, "The higher forms of love break down the narrow self-regarding motives" (*AI* 288).

Whitehead made much of that "Harmony of Harmonies" which he called "Peace." "Thus Peace," he explained,

> is self-control at its widest,—at the width where the 'self' has been lost, and interest has been transferred to coordinations wider than personality. Here the real motive interests of the spirit are meant, and not the superficial play of discursive ideas. (*AI* 285)

Many spiritualists speak of "self-loss" and "self-emptying," but this can and should be seen as a complement to indirect "self-gain" and "self-fullfilling."

Identification spirituality, developed and applied in greater depth elsewhere (Edwards, 2012a and 2012b), says that spiritual development and practice at their best move toward loving and identifying ourselves with all in all, thereby taking all goodness into ourselves and making it our own, as it is God's own. When we find ourselves by losing ourselves within the goodness of all in all, our older, narrow, exclusivist, and self-centered self disappears. We are emptied of that. But by serendipity we gain a new loving self that through identification includes all goodness in all; we become a self that is full of content, not empty of all content. Identification-spirituality is "new self" spirituality, not the "no self" spirituality of some mystics. This is a spirituality of fullness, not of emptiness. At the pinnacle of axiological self-development, the ethical self and the spiritual self are experientially indistinguishable.

In conclusion, consider Robert S. Hartman's description of saints.

> Indeed, geniuses in axiology may well be saints, "saint" being defined as an axiological genius both in knowledge and action. To be a saint is a profession, like any other; it is the identification of self with every self.

> The more intelligent a person is the better he or she will know how to value, for the more and wider concepts he or she considers; the most intelligent sees all sub species aeternitas. The narrower one is, seeing more and more of less and less, as does the specialized scientist, . . . the less will one be able to value. The saint is the genius of intrinsic valuation, of ethics, applied to people.

> Only saints can fully live [the] infinite range of the self. A saint is a person who puts his whole power, all the resources of himself, into his own goodness, a man who has discovered his oneness with all creation, all men, all animals, even all things. He lives within the depth of everybody and everything. He is a man of infinite compassion. The deepest intrinsic goodness is to live so deeply and transparently within ourselves that we live deeply and

compassionately with every human being, indeed every living being, indeed, every being. As St. Francis said to Brother Leo when he tried to extinguish the fire on St. Francis' coat: "Brother Leo, be careful with Brother Fire." Or as Albert Schweitzer, who felt pain at having to kill the bacteria when he did an operation. Compassion is one touchstone of moral value. (1995, 86)

WORKS CITED

Belaief, Lynne. *Toward a Whiteheadian Ethics.* Lanham, MD: University Press of America, 1984.

Boethius. *The Theological Tracts.* H.F. Stewart and E.K. Rand, trans. London: Heinemann, 1913.

Bracken, Joseph A. *Christianity and Process Thought.* Philadelphia: Templeton Foundation Press, 2006.

___. "Continuity Amid Discontinuity: A Neo-Whiteheadian Understanding of the Self." *Process Studies* 31.2 (2002): 115-24.

___. "Energy-Events and Fields." *Process Studies* 18.3 (1989): 153-65.

___. "Panentheism: A Field-Oriented Approach." Philip Clayton and Arthur Peacocke, eds. In *Whom We live and Move and Have Our Being: Panentheistic Reflections on God's Presence in a Scientific World.* Grand Rapids: Wm. B Eerdmans, 2004. 211-21.

Cobb, John B., Jr. *A Christian Natural Theology: Based on the Thought of Alfred North Whitehead.* Philadelphia: Westminster Press, 1965.

___. *Is It Too Late? A Theology of Ecology.* Beverly Hills: Bruce, 1972.

___. *Matters of Life and Death.* Louisville, KY: Westminster/John Knox Press, 1991.

___. *Spiritual Bankruptcy.* Nashville: Abingdon Press, 2010.

Cobb, Jr., John B., Bruce G. Epperly, and Paul S. Nancarrow. *The Call of the Spirit: Process Spirituality in a Relational World.* Claremont, CA: P&F Press, 2005.

Daly, Herman E., and John B. Cobb, Jr. *For the Common Good,* Boston: Beacon Press, 1994.

Dicken, Thomas M., and Rem B. Edwards. *Dialogues on Values and*

Centers of Value. Amsterdam/New York: Editions Rodopi, 2001.

Dombrowski, Daniel A. *Babies and Beasts: The Argument from Marginal Cases*. Champaign: University of Illinois Press, 1997.

___. *Hartshorne and the Metaphysics of Animal Rights*. Albany: State University of New York Press, 1988.

___. "The Replaceability Argument." *Process Studies* 30.1 (2001): 22-35.

Edwards, Rem B. *Animals and Ethics*. Two audiotapes. I wrote the text. First Robert Guillaume then Cliff Robertson were celebrity readers. Knowledge Products, Nashville, TN, Knowledge Products, 1995.

___. "God and Process." James F. Harris, ed. *Logic, God, and Metaphysics*. Dordrecht/Boston/London: Kluwer Academic Publishers, 1992. 41-57.

___. "God as a Processing Actual Entity." *Process Studies*, forthcoming, 2013a.

___. *John Wesley's Values—And Ours*. Lexington, KY: Emeth Press, 2012a.

___. "Minimizing Utilitarianism: An Ethical Theory for Clinical Practice." Rem B. Edwards and E. Edward Bittar. *Advances in Bioethics: Bioethics for Medical Education*. Stamford, CT: JAI Press, 1999.

___. "People and Their Worth: Uniting Process and Axiology." *Process Studies* 38.1 (2009): 43-68.

___. "Some Spurious Proofs for the Pure Ego." Rem B. Edwards, ed. *Formal Axiology and Its Critics*. Amsterdam/Atlanta: Editions Rodopi, 1995. 41-50.

___. *Spiritual Values and Evaluations*. Lexington, KY: Emeth Press, 2012b.

___. *The Essentials of Formal Axiology*. Lanham, MD: University Press of America, 2010.

___. "The Value of Man in the Hartman Value System." *The Journal of Value Inquiry* 3 (1973): 141-47.

___. "The Human Self: An Actual Entity or a Society?" *Process Studies* 5

(1975): 195-203.

___. "The Principle of Utility and Mill's Minimizing Utilitarianism." *The Journal of Value Inquiry* 20 (1986): 125-36.

___. "Toward an Axiological Virtue Ethics." *Quarterly of Ethical Research* 3 (2013b): 25-60. An Islamic philosophy journal sponsored by the departments of theology and philosophy at the University of Qom, Iran.

___. "Universals, Individuals, and Intrinsic Goods." Rem B. Edwards and John W. Davis, eds. *Forms of Value and Valuation, Theory and Applications.* Lanham, MD: University Press of America, 1991. 81-104.

___. *What Caused the Big Bang?* Amsterdam/New York: Editions Rodopi, 2001.

Edwards, Rem B., and Graber, Glenn C. *Bio-Ethics.* San Diego: Harcourt Brace Jovanovich, 1988.

Ford, Lewis. "Enduring Subjectivity." *Process Studies* 35 (2006): 291-318.

Goheen, John. "Whitehead's Theory of Value." Paul Arthur Schilpp, ed. *The Philosophy of Alfred North Whitehead.* La Salle, IL: Open Court, 1941. 437-59.

Gray, James R. *Process Ethics.* Lanham, MD: University Press of America, 1983.

Griffin, David. *God & Religion in the Postmodern World.* Albany: State University of New York Press, 1989.

___. *The Reenchantment of Science.* Albany: State University of New York Press, 1988.

___. *Religion and Scientific Naturalism: Overcoming the Conflicts.* Albany: State University of New York Press, 2000.

Hartman Institute. <http://www.hartmaninstitute.org>.

Hartman, Robert S. *Freedom to Live: The Robert Hartman Story.* Amsterdam/Atlanta: Rodopi, 1994. Second edition, 2013. Robert S.

Hartman Institute.

———. "Formal Axiology and Its Critics." Rem B. Edwards, ed. *Formal Axiology and Its Critics.* Amsterdam/Atlanta: Editions Rodopi, 1995. 51-141.

———. "The Nature of Valuation." Rem B. Edwards and John W. Davis, eds. *Forms of Value and Valuation: Theory and Applications.* Lanham, MD: University Press of America, 1991. 9-35.

———. "The Self in Kierkegaard." *Journal of Existential Psychiatry* 8 (1962): 409-36.

———. *The Structure of Value.* Carbondale and Edwardsville, IL: Southern Illinois University Press, 1967. Republished in 2011 by Wipf & Stock, Eugene, OR.

———. "Singular and Particular." *Critica* 2 (1968): 15-51.

———. "Sputnik's Moral Challenge." *The Texas Quarterly* 3 (1960): 9-23.

———."The Value Structure of Creativity. *The Journal of Value Inquiry* 6 (1972): 243-79.

———. "Value Propositions." Ray Lepley, ed *The Language of Value.* New York: Columbia University Press, 1957. 197-231.

Hartshorne, Charles. *Anselm's Discovery: A Re-examination of the Ontological Proof for God's Existence.* La Salle: Open Court, 1965.

———. *Creative Synthesis & Philosophic Method.* La Salle: Open Court, 1970.

———. *The Divine Relativity.* New Haven: Yale University Press, 1948.

———. *Reality as Social Process: Studies in Metaphysics and Religion.* Glencoe, IL: The Free Press, 1953.

———. *Whitehead's Philosophy: Selected Essays, 1935-1970.* Lincoln, NE: University of Nebraska Press, 1972.

Henning, Brian. *The Ethics of Creativity.* Pittsburgh: University of Pittsburgh Press, 2005.

Kant, I. *Foundations of the Metaphysics of Morals.* Indianapolis: Bobbs-

Merrill, 1969.

Moore, G.E. *Principia Ethica.* Cambridge: The University Press, 1903.

Oord, Thomas Jay. *The Nature of Love: A Theology.* St. Louis: Chalice Press, 2010.

Singer, Peter. *Animal Liberation.* New York: New York Review Books, 1975.

Schilpp, Paul Arthur. "Whitehead's Moral Philosophy." Paul Arthur Schilpp, ed. *The Philosophy of Alfred North Whitehead.* La Salle, IL: Open Court, 1941. 563-618.

Whitehead, Alfred North. *Adventures of Ideas (AI).* New York: The Free Press, 1961.

___. *Modes of Thought (MT).* New York: The Free Press, 1968.

___. *Process and Reality (PR).* Corrected Edition. D.W. Sherburne and D.R. Griffin, eds. New York: The Free Press, 1978.

___. *Religion in the Making (RM).* New York: Macmillan, 1926.

___. *Science and the Modern World (SMW).* New York: The Free Press, 1953.

___. *The Aims of Education (AE).* New York: Free Press, 1967.

___. *The Concept of Nature (CN).* Cambridge: The University Press, 1971.

___. *The Function of Reason (FR).* Princeton: Princeton University Press, 1929.

___. *The Interpretation of Science: Selected Essays (IS).* A.H. Johnson, ed. Indianapolis: Bobbs-Merrill, 1961.

___. *Essays in Science and Philosophy (SP).* New York: Philosophical Library, 1947.

ABOUT THE AUTHOR

REM B. EDWARDS, Ph.D., grew up in the small town of Crawfordville, GA. He attended Emory at Oxford, then graduated as a philosophy major from Emory University with an A.B. degree in 1956. There he was elected to Phi Beta Kappa. Throughout graduate school, he was a Danforth Graduate Fellow, which paid for all his graduate education. He received a B.D. degree from Yale University Divinity School (YDS) in 1959 and a Ph.D. in Philosophy from Emory University in 1962, where he studied under Charles Hartshorne. While at YDS, during the summer of 1958, he was the minister at Old Brick Church Congregational in Clarendon, VT. After finishing YDS, he served for a year as the minister of Dixie Methodist Church in LaGrange, GA. After completing his Ph.D. at Emory, he taught for four years at Jacksonville University in Florida, moved from there to the University of Tennessee in 1966, and retired from there partly in 1997 and partly in 1998. He kept an office on the university campus until the end of May 2000. He was a U. T. Chancellor's Research Scholar in 1985 and a distinguished Lindsay Young Professor between 1987-98. He continues to be professionally active.

His areas of specialization are philosophy of religion, American philosophy, medical ethics, and ethical theory, with a special focus on mental health care ethics, ethics and animals, and formal axiology.

He has published twenty-one other books including *Reason and Religion* (New York: Harcourt, 1972 and Lanham, MD: University Press of America, 1979); *Pleasures and Pains: A Theory of Qualitative Hedonism* (Ithaca: Cornell University Press, 1979); with Glenn Graber, *BioEthics* (San Diego: Harcourt, 1988); with John W. Davis, *Forms of Value and*

Valuation: Theory and Applications (Lanham, MD: University Press of America, 1991); *Formal Axiology and Its Critics* (Amsterdam & Atlanta: Rodopi, 1995); *Violence, Neglect, and the Elderly,* co-edited with Roy Cebik, Glenn Graber, and Frank H. Marsh (Greenwich, CT: JAI Press, 1996); *New Essays on Abortion and Bioethics* (Greenwich, CT: JAI Press, 1997); *Ethics of Psychiatry: Insanity, Rational Autonomy, and Mental Health Care* (Buffalo, NY: Prometheus Books, 1997); *Values, Ethics, and Alcoholism,* co-edited with Wayne Shelton (Greenwich, CT: JAI Press, 1997); *Bioethics for Medical Education,* co-edited with Dr. Edward Bittar (Stamford, CT: JAI Press, 1999); *Dialogues on Values and Centers of Value* (Amsterdam & New York: Rodopi, 2001), co-authored with Thomas M. Dicken; and *What Caused the Big Bang?* (Amsterdam & New York: Rodopi, 2001). *What Caused the Big Bang* received the "Best Book of 2001" award from the Editors of the Value Inquiry Book Series. His T*he Essentials of Formal Axiology* was published in 2010 by the University Press of America. Published by Emeth Press in 2012 were his *John Wesley's Values—And Ours* and his *Spiritual Values and Evaluations*. Edwards has also authored ninety articles and reviews.

He is an Associate Editor with the Value Inquiry Book Series, published by Rodopi, where he is responsible for the Hartman Institute Axiological Studies special series. For a number of years he was co-editor of the Advances in Bioethics book series published by JAI Press. He also did significant editorial work on the following books published in Rodopi's Hartman Institute Axiological Studies: Frank G. Forrest, *Valuemetrics: The Science of Personal and Professional Ethics*, 1994; Robert S. Hartman, *Freedom to Live: The Robert Hartman Story*, 1994; Armando Molina, *Our Ways: Values and Character*, 1997; Gary Acquaviva, *Violence, Values, and Our Future*, 2000; Robert S. Hartman, *The Knowledge of Good*, 2002, co-edited with Arthur Ellis; Leon Pomeroy, *The New Science of Axiological*

Psychology, 2005; Gary Gallopin, *Beyond Perestroika: Axiology and the New Russian Entrepreneurs,* 2009. In 2008, Edwards became the senior editor of the new *Journal of Formal Axiology: Theory and Practice.*

Edwards has been the President of the Tennessee Philosophical Association (1973-74), the Society for Philosophy of Religion (1981-82), and the Southern Society for Philosophy and Psychology, (1984-85). He is a Charter Member and Fellow of the Robert S. Hartman Institute for Formal and Applied Axiology and has served on its Board of Directors since 1987. In 1989 he became its Secretary/Treasurer; after October of 2007, he continued as its Secretary until October 2009, and is now the Contact Secretary. He has been a Webmaster for the website of the Robert S. Hartman Institute at: http://www.hartmaninstitute.org. He is a lifelong Methodist.